AUTOBIOGRAPHY
of a GENERATION

AUTOBIOGRAPHY

of a GENERATION

ITALY, 1968

Luisa Passerini

Translated by Lisa Erdberg

Foreword by Joan Wallach Scott

Wesleyan University Press

Middletown, Connecticut

Published by Wesleyan University Press, Middletown, CT 06459

© 1996 by Wesleyan University Press

Originally published as *Autoritratto di gruppo* by Luisa Passerini

© 1988, 1994 by Giunti Gruppo Editoriale, Firenze

First Wesleyan paperback 2004

Printed in the United States of America

5   4   3

CIP data appear at the end of the book

When you have a past, Yvonne, you'll realize what a curious thing it is. First of all, there are whole corners in there, of landslides: where there's nothing left. Elsewhere, weeds that have grown at random, and one can no longer make sense of anything there either. And then there are spots that seem so beautiful that one repaints them for himself every year, in one color one time, another color another time, and there it ends up no longer looking anything like what it was. Not to mention what one believed very simply and without any mystery when it happened, and that then years later reveals itself to be not nearly so clear as it seemed, just as sometimes you may spend all your time at some ordinary business without paying any attention to it and then all of a sudden you're aware of it.

—Raymond Queneau

CONTENTS

TRANSLATOR'S NOTE

Translating is inherently frustrating. It is also perilous, as the Italian expression *traduttore/traditore*—translator/traitor—succinctly admonishes. But while the peril is constant and certain problems are recurrent, each text holds its own pitfalls, and the present work is no exception.

In translating *Autobiography of a Generation* I encountered two distinct but related problems that, in a certain sense, reflect the structure and nature of the book. The first difficulty was capturing the undercurrent of playfulness running through an essentially serious, and sometimes sad, book. This playfulness manifests itself not only in explicit discussion of the importance of wit and humor in the student movement and descriptions of particular jokes and pranks but also more generally through figurative language whose subtleties don't always survive the process of translation.

The second difficulty also involved capturing a playful spirit, but this one was even more elusive—the unconscious at play. The multiple meanings of dream images and associations stimulated by the psychoanalytic process, and their expression—especially in the experience of a well-educated, polyglot subject like the author, already accustomed to playing with words—raised difficult, and in some cases insurmountable, problems. I only hope that as much was found as was lost in translation. My goal was to recreate as accurately as possible the tone of the original, both the author's voice in the autobiographical chapters and the voices of the various narrating subjects in the "historical" chapters. I have, as a result, stayed very close to the Italian in my translation.

This undertaking was unexpectedly moving for me, perhaps because my own experiences of the sixties and seventies in many respects parallel Luisa Passerini's. I am grateful to her for her interest in and collaboration on this translation, and I only regret that time constraints severely limited the extent of that collaboration. I hope that I have betrayed neither her trust nor her text.

—Lisa M. Erdberg

San Francisco
September 1995

FOREWORD

Luisa Passerini is not an ordinary historian. She seeks instead to push the boundaries of history beyond what they have been conventionally. While others have read individual and collective actions as the reflection of economic structures or cultural institutions, Passerini has argued for greater interpretive complexity. Her work insists at once on the specificity and complexity of individual subjectivities and on their historicity. This means accepting the fact that there is always "tension between individual reality and general process. . . . [T]he psychological realm can never be completely deduced from social experience, but stands in a polar relation to it—both opposed and linked to it."[1] One of her continuing preoccupations has been with developing methods for turning this insight into historical practice. "It is an irony of history," she wrote in 1984, "that what is written about it so largely ignores the personal lives of individuals in the very period (the past hundred years) when individual subjectivity has been transformed, becoming an important area of scientific study and political interest. It seems vital that historical research, too, should join other disciplines in recognizing the importance of such developments."[2]

Passerini has been a pioneer in the study of the history of subjectivity. She has examined the impact of social and cultural change in Africa and in Italy; she has analyzed the sources and uses of memory for historical analysis; and she has explored the relationship between memory, subjectivity, and history. Her contributions to discussions of method in oral history have been innovative (earning her a position from 1984 to 1993 as an associate professor of the methodology of history at the University of Turin. She is currently Professor of History at the European University in Florence). She uses interviews not

1. Luisa Passerini, *Fascism in Popular Memory: The Cultural Experience of the Turin Working Class,* trans. by Robert Lumley and Jude Bloomfeld (Cambridge: Cambridge University Press, 1987), p. 11.
2. Ibid., p. 3.

to collect facts, not to clarify what did and did not happen in the past, but to explore the ways in which the relationship between private and public, personal and political is negotiated. It is this negotiation that produces identity, the sense of membership in a collective whether it is "women," "the working class," or the "generation of 1968." Memory, Passerini suggests, sustains identity through its invocation of a common history. The point for the historian is not to take memory literally, but to analyze its operations in the formation of identity.

> Memory narrates in the vivid tones of actual experience. But what interests me is neither the liveliness of the accounts nor their faithfulness to reality, both of which would make these stories a secondary source for a good social history of Italy after 1945. Rather, what attracts me is memory's insistence on creating a history of itself, which is much less and perhaps somewhat more than a social history. (p. 23)

"Much less and somewhat more than a social history" is a good description of *Autobiography of a Generation: Italy, 1968.* In it, Passerini probes the phenomenon of memory from many different perspectives. She uses her own psychoanalysis to think about memory not only as a rational recollection of past experience (it is in part that), but also as a repository of unconscious impressions, repressed emotions and desires, deferred fantasies. Indeed, when viewed through the lens of psychoanalysis, what is rationally remembered is not a simple reflection of social position, economic structure, or political event; it is instead a way of selectively organizing experience to produce and explain one's self. Analysis probes the selections, teasing out repressed elements and silences by reading symbols and metaphors, looking for contradictions and ruptures in narratives, listening for denials and displacements, asking questions about feeling.

Passerini uses these methods to interpret the oral histories she has collected, but not in order to psychoanalyze the generation of students from Turin who participated in the events of 1968. What is so compelling about this book is precisely that it avoids the reductive "psychohistory" that applies Freudian explanatory labels (such as "family romance" or "Oedipal struggle") to collective behavior. In contrast, Passerini reads analytically, and this allows her to elicit historically specific patterns from her material. Attentive to contradiction, ambiguity, and paradox, she allows the words of her subjects to provide insight into the complexity of their subjectivity. Thus, she points out the paradoxical fact that identity "must assert itself as antihistorical" (that is, as something fixed, immutable, inherent) in order to become history (that is, personally or politically visible and efficacious) (p. 24). Thus she notes the contradictory love/hate relationship that so many of her subjects had to learning and to books (p. 68). Thus she identifies themes of mourning and loss in the retrospective accounts given by '68ers, and she ties these to the question of power. "It is precisely the demise of the question of power that is the central grief hanging over the entire seventies and casting its long shadow on us still." The question of power "was a way of recognizing transcendence, in the secular sense," in the sense of being able to influence the march of history. That power could be addressed in daily life, as well as in formal politics, meant that one made "a constant effort to participate in reality and to understand it" (p. 132). All aspects of life seemed linked by one's ethical and political commitments. The loss of that sense of connection is manifest differently in different individuals, but it is nonetheless a collective historical experience.

Autobiography of a Generation consists of three different but interconnected exercises. There is a running account of Passerini's analysis. There are the personal memories the analysis provokes—of her childhood, her adulthood, her participation in the events of 1968. And there are the life stories told by those who were activist students in Turin in 1968. The accounts overlap and intertwine; insights gained in one area nurture insights in another. Without the life stories, Passerini's account might have acquired the narcissistic aspect of the "confessional" literature so much in vogue these days among literary critics in the United States. But in her book, the life stories of others provide a context for and a commentary on her own. The whole does not, however, add up to a social or cultural history in the sense of a documented narrative of the causes and effects of the events of 1968. Nor is it the kind of collective history of "mentalités" we have come to associate with the Annales school. In its attention to individual specificity and to collective memory, to the construction and experience of subjectivity, Luisa Passerini's book captures something that is, arguably, closer to lived history than anything we are accustomed to reading. It demonstrates not only that a history of subjectivity is possible, but also that psychoanalysis can enable the writing of such a history. It demonstrates, as well, that the history of politics takes on new dimensions when subjectivity, in all its complicated and contradictory manifestations, is taken into account with the kind of reading Passerini provides.

Toward the end of the book, Passerini reflects on what she has accomplished. Her words can serve as a conclusion to this preface and as an introduction to her book:

> Only now is the complementary nature of my two undertakings evident. If I had not heard the life stories of the generation of '68, I would not have been able to write about myself; these stories have nourished mine, giving it the strength to get to its feet and to speak. But I couldn't have borne them, in their alternation of being too full and too empty, if I had not confronted myself and my history with the double motion of analysis and of the exercise of remembering. (p. 124)

At once an individual and a collective autobiography, this book is innovative in its method, fascinating and instructive in its substance; it is a novel and compelling history.

Princeton, New Jersey —Joan Wallach Scott

AUTOBIOGRAPHY
of a GENERATION

Mirrors

JANUARY

I conducted my first interviews with the protagonists of '68. The interviews plunge me into my own past: as I listen, the film of what I was doing at the time unreels. Memory redoubled in this way is hard to bear; it seems to me that until now no one has wanted to take on this burden, sometimes not even those who tell their stories. The mirror I see my image reflected in is opaque. My interviews with the elderly about their memories of Fascism had absorbed and moved me, but they weren't so weighty, so unresolved, so enigmatic.

FEBRUARY

Birthday spent in bed with a fever. I lie defeated, under the weight of my own contradictions. I didn't want children, and I won't have any. The man who had been living with me for ten years has definitively settled in the city he had been commuting to, taking seriously my earlier requests that we live separately, just now when I need him here; he has left only armoires full of clothes, books, objects. The book I worked on for so many years, on the memory of Fascism, appeared for a few days in the windows of two or three bookstores, and quickly disappeared.
I began a relationship with a man twenty years younger and this is the result; my fever tells me it can't go on like this. I feel like someone who has run out of cards to play.

Phone calls in search of trustworthy psychoanalysts. One appointment in which we both seem to be asking each other what we're doing here in this office. More phone calls. At the other end of one a fine, deep voice answers. Having learned from experience, I make it clear that my request is for an appointment right away. The voice grasps the urgency and counters: it may be possible, a place has just opened up. Appointment for next month.

MARCH

My initial reaction to the transcripts of the first interviews is that they are unusable. They reproduce neither my own emotion at seeing myself in the mirror nor that of the other person at recounting his or her own experience as a whole for the first time. Those who get the transcripts react with disappointment, irritation, rejection. They correct meticulously, adding commas and marking out the "uh's" and "that is's." Some choose pseudonyms, others refuse authorization to use the interview; many ask me what I expect to get out of the interviews. The comparison with one's memory, and with the transition from spoken to written, is discouraging. I had already intuited that it would be necessary to wrest this memory from its own protagonists.

I had my first meeting with Dr. G.
Modest appearance—was I perhaps expecting something grandiose? All the while I was claiming urgency I was emphasizing my lack of time and money. G. proposed trial meetings until Easter, saying that he discerned an emotional stirring, but not a clear demand for analysis.

APRIL

I'm in Venice for an interview. The house has warped floors, which quiver at every step and slope toward the canal. Every day we tape for hours—I'm the guest of my interviewee. In his story I observe some of my own experiences; in his gestures I recognize some of my passions. He eats only once a day, bringing a certain asceticism to his pleasure in food and wine. I listen to his prison experiences; despite the differences, I sense an affinity to periods of confinement in my own solitude.

In Venice I dreamed about a quartet: at the sides two men are watching, one on the left and one on the right; in the center, a slender girl squatting, her back to me, is looking at a full-figured, imposing woman, mature breasts and belly, who is rising to her feet, taking shape, in front. She is still not fully erect, her nudity is bursting forth, rich, almost excessive. A potent image. Some nights later, a similar promise, of which only a faint echo stays with me, barely perceptible: a woman shaped like a pear, and the pear is transparent, like a veil, a glass bell, the aureole of fireflies under an overturned glass in the dark woods. But by now these are images created by the mind. Back there, in that remote barren plain, was a slow shedding of skins, like an onion—back, back, you almost can't capture it with the eye—one woman inside another, one woman through another. Fairy tale about the beautiful Maria made of wood, tossed in the river, her pretty clothes hidden by the armor that completely covers her and that she will only remove for love.

I relate my dreams to Dr. G. In the preceding weeks I had been quite worried about the fate of my analysis. The problem of money was an ongoing embarrassment and torment to me; at my age, not even to be able to afford to pay for analysis without difficulty seemed like a checkmate, another sign of my dissipation—of resources and energy. Now, all this receded in the face of the announcement, made by the dreams, of a possible new woman, pregnant with things and with herself.

The decision made itself, or the dreams made it.

MAY

I do mental exercises as soon as I wake up to recapture my dreams; I review them without putting them into words, to be certain of getting them firmly fixed. When I sit down in the small, wicker armchair a few yards from G., who waits, I always begin with my dreams. An overflow of colors and images, which I zealously pour out for him, without understanding the relevances, the differences, without any separation between dream and reality. I would love to phone the people I dream about, to see them, to touch them.
Consolation, to alternate luminous and brightly colored nights, transported by a sense of adventure, with solitary, sad, repetitive days. It's pleasant to share my dreams with G.
Walking through the streets, my dreams keep me company. Smells hav-

ing no clear material source emerge: hyacinths, strawberries. I feel as if my head were wreathed in garlands of flowers and foliage.

After some weeks the dreams become known, evocable. Signs of structure, occurrences and recurrences, take shape in the formless mass. But the totality makes a mockery of interpretation. Nor do we attempt it; I talk, G. listens. Slowly I acquire the sense of an inner space. Frequently I dream about the main piazza of my native city, the city of my childhood and adolescence: distinction between this internal piazza, which I perceive "within and way back," and the image of the actual piazza, which I can summon in my mind's eye. In writing or recounting dreams, in putting them into words, a crossing from one plane to the other takes place, but it's a two-way crossing.

I deliver to G. my stereotypes regarding my origins, more out of a sense of duty than anything else, almost like a letter of introduction one presents without emotion:

"I have no roots, I have no memory of any origins that resemble me. My mother is an absence. I have only negative memories of her:
someone who gets irked because she can't get my straight hair to curl with her curling iron
who gets annoyed because I won't tell her whether there's any mail or not, humming to spite her
someone who goes out, dressed in evening clothes, very elegant, on my father's arm, and I gaze at them from the window until they turn the corner
someone who argues mercilessly with her mother, my grandmother. These scenes take place before I was five. She died when I was six, after long spells in the hospital."
G. listened attentively: "They're like withered roots." "There's been a mutilation," I lament. "No, an atrophy."

A young researcher interviews me. Like me, he is working on the social and political movements of the last two decades, but on a different topic (and I, what topic am I working on?). Like my interviewees, I, too, anecdotally narrated my commonplaces, with improvised attempts at explanation. A strange situation, being asked for one's life story: in a certain sense one is always awaiting this opportunity, but it is both too much and too little for what there is to say. I was also shocked by how much I said without hesitation, without embarrassment, and how sincerely, at least on a conscious level.

The interview stimulated my memory, which doesn't stand still after the
conversation. It keeps going, summoning up images of the most distant,
lost, closed-off part of the past: the happy part, where stories heard a
thousand times are mixed together with childhood memories, before the
separations and the losses.

*In my mother's family—artisans and tradesmen, after the peasant stock
of my great-grandparents, from the Langhe on one side and Monferrato
on the other—the women did everything, they assumed every responsibility, while the men hovered in the background, weaklings or idlers or
miscreants. The tradition included a great-grandfather who went out for
a drink and never returned; he left his wife and five children in Italy to
emigrate to South America, where he was never heard from again. My
grandfather, on the other hand, had died very young, of the Spanish flu
during the First World War, leaving his wife pregnant and with a young
daughter.*
*There were positive male figures, twin great-uncles who lived far away:
one was a cabinetmaker who made fabulous furniture for my dolls; the
other was a pastry chef. There was a story that for Easter once he had sent
a gigantic chocolate egg containing train tickets for everybody and an invitation: "Come visit us" (he lived in Genoa). But these were mythical
images, not everyday ones. The norm was otherwise, and was not belied
by my father's family, a bit blurry, of Ligurian and possibly Central Italian
origins, decimated by diseases and the war. Legend had it that my father
was a soccer player, but that my mother's family had plucked him from
vagrancy (that's how they thought of that sport), forced him to get a degree and settled him in an office job. The fact that he worked as an em-
ployee didn't blot out his original image of adventure and freedom.*
*As a little girl, I got the impression from these stories that it was men's fate
to wander and disappear; women stayed put, survived, hardened under
the burden of responsibility. Mine was a race of tough, intelligent, capable Piedmontese women. Women accustomed to giving orders, to taking
risks, to exercising economic power, who transmitted a message: every
bond with a man is ill-fated; the best that can come of it is children, and
when all is said and done, you're better off without them too.*

I had been born in my grandmother's house, "brought" as they used to
say in those days, by an old midwife, who visited us often, wrapped in a
dark brown overcoat, tall and thin, with a robotic gait. "Madama" Oberti,
who called my grandmother "Madamin" since she was younger, spoke in
a shrill, broken voice. She didn't call me by name, but rather by a generic
affectionate designation, such as "giuìin," little joy; under her gaze I felt

myself return to an endless lineup of those she had delivered, forever children and lacking individuality. Of course she had no husband; she had had one, but he too had disappeared, according to the norm.

In the old house my grandmother's dressmaking studio still existed, reduced now to minimal proportions after having been an atelier with eighteen workers. Yet it was always that culture I absorbed without premeditation, by osmosis: the words mediated by French, like paramentura, sciancrato, pince, the names of fabrics with the accents rewritten and masculinized compared to the original: gàbarden, pòplin, crèp. There was plissé that one wore for going to the big city, the full godé of the big flared skirts, the nido d'ape for the carré of baby clothes. And the songs that the girls sang while they worked, often opera arias, the jokes, the laughter in which my grandmother joined. She alone knew how to do certain things, like cutting; I remember when she would set about doing it, marking the material with tailor's chalk and scorning anyone who used paper patterns; professional, creative, quick.

We had a huge terrace, with a veranda, full of plants and flowers—it was a big job to water the pots in the summer and to sweep the snow in the winter; I stayed there for hours watching the ants, I even knew the cracks in the tiles. The terrace overlooked a large, square courtyard; from the balconies that encircled it flew greetings and news. In order to avoid climbing four flights of steep, wide steps—it was an eighteenth-century building—a lot of people who came looking for us hollered or whistled from the courtyard; we looked out and talked to them and, sometimes, had them come up. It was a way of announcing yourself or of taking care of small matters you use the phone for these days. I vaguely recall that in the early years the ice man, the rag seller, and the glass man also came around. We led a sort of communal life with some of our neighbors: every day they came by to have coffee, to relate a dream, to gossip. I was sent to deliver a taste of some just-cooked dish, to borrow an onion, a cup of sugar, a couple of matches. When we bought our refrigerator and installed our telephone, the neighbors came to inspect and comment.

We spent the summers in the house in the country, which still had wooden balconies and a wood-burning oven for baking bread. In the courtyard, my great-grandmother, still waiting for the husband who had disappeared, spent days cooking huge pots of conserves, of marmalade, of mostarda, which was a grape-based compote, inimitable. To go back to the city they took us in the wagon—luminous dawn over the hill—to catch the bus at the peach market. We carried baskets of tree-ripened peaches with us, tiny, white, perfumed.

They used to tell me fairy tales, always the same ones, which I listened to endlessly, especially the one about Belinda, whose father, in order to satisfy her wish for a white rose (while her sisters wished for gold and silver), stole one from the monster's garden and had to promise his daughter in return. I could see the monster's house, full of all sorts of wonderful things, with the servants who were invisible except for their hands; the magic ring, which darkened when the monster was sick, but which the sisters stole from Belinda out of envy—a dream reminded her that the monster was dying; Belinda who had the courage to kiss him. I imagined his transformation. White roses stood out over everything, the white roses that, at first glance, seemed like the most humble request, and instead had set the whole story in motion.

JUNE

Repeated dreams in which a trip is supposed to begin, but it's already late afternoon, almost evening; how to set off in the dark and for parts unknown? maybe I've started analysis too late? I'm too old?
For the first time G. says something: "The trip could be a descent."
I start with disbelief, dismay.
He observes that I have a childish notion of travel, as heroic, sunny adventure.

Interviews in Milan. One appointment is on the steps of the Duomo, but we didn't anticipate that the former student leader Mario Capanna, now a member of Parliament, would be holding a political rally right there. The past pursues us.

I dream about a gray, opaque, turbulent sea. I am swimming in muddy water near a drainpipe, from which I can't get away. Dr. G.: don't dismiss your resistances; understand their nature. His calmness, the tone of assuredness with which he points out that I'm afraid of the shapeless, the obscure, strike me. Examined in the light of this realistic observation, my terror readjusts to proper proportions. In everyday life I am on edge. I notice squeaks in the furniture, things fall, move, creak behind my back.

Now it is clear, in contrast, that the first three months were a "sky-blue" period, as if I were soaring, borne on the wings of planes, birds, flowers, and mountains. I experienced a sense of speed, almost of dizziness, of being "launched"; at times it seemed to me that I wasn't up to it, that I was flying too high. I was in the sky with my thoughts as well. Bits of verses whirled in my head: "He who dines on heavenly fare has no need of mortal fare," the Commendatore to Don Giovanni; "and everything is flame and blue," Carducci. And memories—in the Conservatory Garden in Central Park, an area covered with blue: mallow, lavender, cornflowers, irises, periwinkles.

Dream: seated on a bed, another person and I are making an inventory of black, dangerous insects, closely laid out on a big card. Spidery legs, spidery letters.
Handwriting: little black legs on a white page, like traces of excrement. The cockroaches also appear in reality, in the night. It happens every year, but never so many as this year. The house is always creaking.

Some friends who moved to the United States came to visit. My old friend and comrade in political struggles is annoyed by the news that I am in analysis. "But you didn't need it." I haven't lived up to my image as a comrade with whom he shared a sense of superiority. He is at his peak: he has a girlfriend twenty years his junior, he travels, he writes, he lives energetically. It's my turn to sink to the bottom, alone. I examine myself carefully for envy, but I don't find any. I'm too attracted by my fate.

In the early morning I found a dying cockroach in the bathroom. The exterminators came, this is the result. I ascertain that I am afraid by the way I inspect my black shawl, where they could burrow; I close drawers and bags, stop up the faucets of the sinks.
I try a scientific approach; in the library I do a little research on cockroaches and blattae, hoping not to be surprised in my endeavor by acquaintances and colleagues. There are thirty species of blattae in Europe, two thousand in the world. They are among the most ancient insects, very important during the Carboniferous Age. In Europe the Blattide Orientalis (20mm, blackish-brown) is overtaking the Phyllodromia Germanica, smaller and lighter. It disgusts me just to look at the illustrations; I can't touch them.

I relate all this to G., who smiles. He mentions the connection between cockroaches and scarabs. I know that he's doing it to find something good even in blattae. No, I counter obstinately, the first belongs to the Coleoptera order, like ladybirds and maybugs, the second belongs to the

Orthoptera along with crickets and grasshoppers. It won't be analysis that will convince me they're alike.

It seems to me that it startles G. slightly when I use technical terms, even "analysis." I stop using them in front of him, making an effort each time to find euphemisms: "our conversations," "these meetings," or more allusive expressions; a gesture to indicate "here."

In London for three days, a meeting for the first comparison of the interviews with the generation of '68. Correspondences only show up between pairs of countries, at most among three countries—similarities between high school education in France and Italy, or certain organizational issues between the United States and Germany, for example. Here too one gets the impression of a memory fleeing from those who would investigate it. Relief from the real cockroaches, but not from those of my dreams, who present themselves regularly, coming out from the bed and then burying themselves in it again. I also dream about two huge babies, white on green grass, who, to my amazement, speak intelligently.

As soon as I'm back home I dream about cockroaches gleaming in the dark. I awaken terrified, I don't dare turn on the light in order not to see the real ones, there on the floor, in their hasty precipitous flight, and then their blind waiting. The glistening of black in the dark like the jackboots of the SS. Black on black. Nazism, Europe/darkness. They will never be innocuous, much less friends. For me they are messengers of darkness, of filth. Dark red almost black with blood.

Netherworld, Hades, otherworld, sewers, slime, darkness, night.

G. takes in my terrors in a playful and mocking spirit. Regarding the huge babies he ventures to say that perhaps I have been doubly struck by the enormous importance of something: that someone who wouldn't know how to talk—the *in-fans*—is talking. In truth, I didn't think that anything within me could speak in such an autonomous, and such an unexpected, voice.

JULY

The infant is very playful. I dreamed that my friend-sister had "zoerrosis." A bit of etymology: it's a made-up word; it could mean, from the ancient Greek, life that flows away, that flees. G. mischievous: well then, it's a chronic condition, "zoerrosis" rather than "zoerritis." The same spirit as the infant. This latter, which I took for mute and ignorant, not only talks; it toys with ancient Greek! With other languages as well, says G. With these discoveries we say good-bye for the vacation.

In Rome, a series of interviews on '68. Once again I run up against the past in an unexpected manner: one of the younger interviewees questions me regarding my situationist period, which he knows something about; an old friend vividly recalls a sad period in which we participated together, the end of New Left politics, in '73. After the interview we stay for a while in the warm night drinking his white wine. I end up telling him about my cockroaches. He nods. He wants to know whether they have a nervous system and what kind. He talks to me, in turn, about polyps.
I have the sensation of traveling underground, I expect encounters with dragons. It amazes me that I can take the plane, the tram, the taxi. I conduct a whole interview without plugging in the microphone, in plain view on the table. The one inside the tape-recorder worked, you just have to disregard the static.
Strong elements of seduction in the narration of one's life. One woman says to me, "I'd like to see you again, not just during an interview." Me too. I tell her bits of my life, I serve as a mirror for her critical moments.

Kos. Grief struck me full bore, without any escape, since I have interrupted my work. I can neither sleep nor stay still for long. For the first time in ten years I am on vacation without a man. I had taken vacations with women before, but by choice, during my feminist phase. Now it is by necessity. Sense of loneliness, of having erred, lost, failed. Shame, tears. But which man do I miss? the last one I had? or any man? pangs of sadness seeing couples with their arms around each other in the streets in the evenings.

Emptiness, sense of my life turned inside out. What I did in the past now appears in a contrary light—I repent of it—politics, my use of time, my travels, meetings. I must expiate, live in death, review everything. Turn upside down, even in my thoughts, what I did and said. My whole life upside down.

The women with me massage my head and shoulders while I cry, they comfort me, they accompany me on walks. At night I go cry on the big terrace with its strongly scented honeysuckle, pots of roses and basil, a small acacia, white carnations, and bougainvillea.
In the morning my friends feed me yogurt and honey. Once upon a time,

in Hades, at the border crossing, the guardian demanded flatbread made
with honey.
The tourists' world represents another hell. Discordant noises, garish
color combinations, uprootedness, obligatory enjoyment. We too join in
one day, taking a trip to Rhodes on the hydrofoil, transportation for the
modern-day netherworld. We all throw up, on the way there and on the
way back.

Along with sleep my dreams have abandoned me as well. Regurgitated
bits of memories, in messy groups, shades of the past emerge. Fixed and
crystallized as they are, why do they hurt so much?

*The entryway under the stairs in my grandmother's old house. The mail-
boxes, where for many years I watched closely for the arrival of who
knows what message, the grate and the wrought-iron gate of the cellar.
During the war when the siren sounded, we went down there as if we
were going to a shelter. My father stayed outside to watch the lights of the
bombardments in the night. That's the way he was, a young hero in my
eyes, handsome, fickle, teasing. He made fun of the fears of my mother's
family, of the orders of those strong, severe women. All except her, my
elegant and beautiful mama. Far away, absent, dead. Perhaps my birth
hastened her demise.*

*Hunger during the war; there was no food, everything was scarce. At one
point we burned a table to keep warm. After the liberation I saw the partisans march by, and women with their skulls painted red.*

*Throughout my childhood there had been two houses: my father's, where
I had lived for several years with him and my mother; my grandmother's
where I had been sent when my mother got too sick. When she disappeared, I had only two feelings: her absence; and being torn between
those who were left, who shared me. In reaction to this abandonment and
division I nurtured a rancor that would last for decades.*

*In the late forties the influence of Fascism was still pervasive in my ele-
mentary school: I remember poems and hymns like "Sun that rises free
and joyful / over our hills your horses rule / you will never see anything
in the world / greater than Rome, greater than Rome."
The teacher instilled in us the cult of Rome, as of a supreme place. The
social distinctions were very clear: the middle-class kids sat in the first
rows, girls and boys in white smocks; in the back were the boys from the*

nearby orphanage, ignorant bad restless, in black smocks; the girls were all in the front rows, whatever their social origins.

The rejects in the back held a particular fascination for me. The first day of school I fell in love with one of them, but after a while he seemed too quiet and the image of another one took over, a kid with a big shock of hair, his blue kerchief always crooked and a mocking grin, who called me "Luisella caramella."

My closest bond was with a girl, my best friend, whom I even saw on Sunday afternoons, when she visited her aunt who lived in the same building as me. We concocted sumptuous snacks together, with hot chocolate and apple tortes. In third grade they took us to Rome together: a night on the train, a day going around the city, another night on the train (which was deserted, we could stretch out in the empty compartments).

At the end of fifth grade the class split in two: for those who were going to vocational school there would be no further opportunities for study; for those who were going on to middle school a world of possibilities opened up. The passage to middle school was the entrance into terror, hard work, sacrifice. The class was strictly single-sex, all of us in black smocks with white collars, lugubriously uniform. The evaluation process was grueling, especially for students who could stay in school only if they did well, like those of us from the lower-middle classes, while the kids of professionals and the wealthy always ended up getting by, what with private tutoring and recommendations. The nightmare of failing, of having to repeat the exams the next fall, or just of getting a bad grade, was unending.

The story of the separate desks constituted part of this reign of terror. My best friend was the daughter of a well-to-do doctor, a Christian Democrat, a Jew converted to Catholicism. We had always shared a desk, but in the seventh grade the humanities teacher separated us, as punishment for a bad Latin assignment.

Daily misery, seeing each other and not being able to be close. The following year, at the beginning of eighth grade, on the first day of school we sat at the same desk. The teacher gave us a terrible look: "You know I don't want to see you together, you two."

In high school, we were reunited and every day for five years we shared one of those old wooden desks where we kept everything in common, objects, emotions, whispers. According to my friend, the reason for the separation in middle school had been a request by her father, unhappy about her too-close friendship with the daughter of a Socialist. It seemed unbelievable to me, my father was hardly a militant. Besides, he had done things for the Resistance, like sending messages, carrying packages —he worked for the railroad—but after the war he had turned down any

official recognition, he had no political ambitions. To be sure, he made
no secret of voting Socialist, of being a supporter of Pietro Nenni.
For me the whole affair of being exiled to separate desks had been an experience of the iniquity of the world. It seemed to me a matter of destiny
that it had been a victim who inflicted on me a punishment dispropor-
tionate to my error. The teacher had been persecuted by the Nazis, she
had lost her family in a concentration camp, she still bore that terrible
mark on her arm. For me, who couldn't see pictures of prisoners in the
camps without trembling, she had been symbolically both victim and
persecutor. I couldn't talk to anyone about that fear and misery. Only occasionally with my friend, but not much, because it hurt too much and
there was nothing to do, no one to ask for help.

Kalimnos, sleepy port, visits to convents. The nuns welcome us festively,
they offer us sweets, ouzo, fried eggplant. Grief is suspended, put off.

SEPTEMBER

I dream about a crowded meeting in a tiered hall, where I am up very
high. Looking down makes me sick; how can I speak from up here? But
going down scares me.
Stop trying to be on top of things. Let myself go, come down from the
platform of the ego, from the aspiration to "be there," to participate, yesterday through politics, today through oral history.
Is this what the dreams mean? I resist, I'm scared, I don't decide.
I don't have anything other than that heroic identity.

I meet with Dr. G. again. It didn't seem as if I had missed him, and now
instead I discover a slight undercurrent of resentment, like a child who
says, "Why were you away?"

Dreamed a giantess in a bar, huge thighs, between which one could
glimpse a sex organ perhaps more male than female, but confused: a
virago. Many dreams about homosexual friends, role reversals between
them and me. What are masculine and feminine? Haven't I been a masculine woman for a long time?

Stretched out for hours on the couch without doing anything. Total loss of
identity. Disorientation, I move slowly, groping my way, vision that dis-
torts objects, pupils that don't focus. I drop things. Fragments of recollec-

tion of when I was alive: I was working on my research on Fascism in the central archives of the EUR, I used to go out at noon to eat a sandwich and an apple in the winter sun.

Why are Saturday nights so hard? Eat without too much haste at a table which is not too messy, with motions that have a certain rhythm: this will preserve at least a bit of dignity. Degradation experienced in these last days, depression, sleepiness at seven in the evening. Get up in the morning with a set idea of when it's okay to go to sleep again. Every day I cross one day off the calendar. Whirlwinds, empty head, palpitations.

Even when I organize my Sundays, like this one, the emptiness expelled by the day reappears at night.

OCTOBER

Memorable session with Dr. G.
"I can no longer go either forward or backward."
Silence.
I resume narrating old dreams, I talk nonsense, I stop. I don't know what to say, other than that I am sick at heart. My mother too had heart sickness.
I have a medical statement that her illness was not hereditary. G. says something to me, I don't know what, and it all converges. A wave of heat rises from my chest to my head, I try to speak, but the thing is out of control. The meeting of our glances is almost unsustainable, we are getting toward the end of the hour, I could get up and run away. I take my head in my hands: "It's something very strong." He motions to me with his cupped hands as if holding something precious: "Hang on to it!"
"What should I do?"
"Don't do anything," joking impatience as if with a slightly dull-witted student.
"It will overwhelm me," I say fearfully.
He gestures no, there's no danger.
I don't try to talk any more.
I look at him every once in a while; I detect com-passion, tenderness, solidarity. He's with me. I sit still, my emotions swirling around me. On leaving, I drop two books. G. shakes my hand warmly, almost as if to congratulate and fortify me. I leave bumping into the doorpost, as in a cartoon.

In Greece, hiking among the ruins and in the mountains, without thinking about it I was searching in all the rocks, in the natural rocks on the beaches as well as in the carved rocks in the excavations and museums. I realized I was looking for a rock to take back to Dr. G. Fortunately I hadn't found any that were sufficiently pretty.

In the heat flash session, the roots of my rancor—the four recollections of my mother recounted at the outset—showed that they weren't totally withered, they moved, swollen with emotion. It was also possible thanks to that look returned by G., a mirror that, from distracted and playful, had become watchful, strong, attentive. For me, who at one time sexualized all relationships, this type of love is ever so precious.

I reread the medical certificate regarding the nonhereditary nature of the physical disease: "myocardial insufficiency with total arrythmia." And yet I have been really sick, for years, with emotional insufficiency and high and low acidities in my affections.

NOVEMBER

Intense period of interviews in Naples. Day takes precedence over night. They're different, these Neapolitan life histories. A grand style of story-telling, a sense of the tragic heightened by laughter; echoes of the recent earthquake; the presence of those more defeated than we, who can't talk about '68 because they're strung out on drugs, emarginated, lost. A dignity in the obligation to narrate. With gentle smiles my interlocutors make certain—politely—that I understand that they're not telling me every-thing, that I am aware of the distance between the story and the truth. I depart with regret for the work someone could do on memory and its narrative in this city.

Almost a year after he left, the man who had been living with me still hasn't come to pick up his belongings. I open the armoires and out tum-ble his sweaters; his shoes clutter up the closet. I throw objects and books in suitcases and trunks, which I send to his mother (is it always between women that such matters get resolved?). I have the nameplates on the doors and doorbells redone and I replace them.

I dreamed I was getting rid of a black and white sack dress and picking out a red one, fitted at the waist and clinging, which was perfect on me.

"I never wear clothes like that," I tell G., worried.

"Just think, red!" he teases.

"But even the style . . . and then I did so much work on red and black in my book on Fascism, but here the connections elude me."

"Not to be interpreting everything all the time," he says, "but one could say that reason, a certain way of understanding reason, proceeds by black and white, by opposition."

The red of passion, on the other hand, is whole.

Another of the discoveries of the "u" (un-conscious, un-speaking): I dream about putting on my white sheepskin coat, being called repeatedly by the teacher "*Signorina Angelini.*" Irresponsible innocence, washing one's hands of practical matters, presenting oneself as *puella,* intellectual without family or emotional obligations, without the ties of the house-wife. Young girl who doesn't get dirty, doesn't mix, doesn't age, like the angels.

DECEMBER

After years, I once again pay attention to how I dress, coordinating colors, accessories, sometimes I even wear make-up. Everyone remarks on it: "You look so elegant." For me, it's a way of demonstrating a femininity, a way of being like my mother.

I talk to G. again about the old dream about "zoerrosis," loss of life, to tell him that such a malady has struck my heroic identity, currently mori-bund. G. responds that in the past that identity itself represented a loss of life. Connections between the heroic part and rigid notions of reason on one side, of passion on the other.

"But I'm not capable of putting on the red dress of passion."

"Who says? In the dream it suits you perfectly."

"The red dress is out of style anyway, it's fitted at the waist."

"What do you mean?"

I explain to him that they're no longer wearing clothes cut like that; the black and white one is straight, shapeless.

"It's lifeless," he smiles, punning on the Italian word *vita* meaning both "life" and "waist."

Accept together darkness and passion, black and red. At birth my mother had been consecrated to the Madonna of Lourdes, so that the Madonna

would preserve her in spite of her bad heart. For this reason, up to the age
of twelve my mother always had to wear blue clothes—all shades of blue,
but only blue. Her clothes that were left to me, which I keep, are red and
black.

I tell G. incidentally that in my father's house—not in my grandmother's
—there were cockroaches. All of a sudden I see them from a different
standpoint, an image comes to mind in which cockroaches in formation
carry a little light on their backs. From earth to heaven or vice versa.

"See?" says G. triumphantly. "Mediators between heaven and earth."
Thus not irremediably inimical, evil, filthy.

Train from Bologna to Turin. Amidst the torpor of the journey a vision in
the corridor of a woman kneeling in front of a newborn. The annunci-
ation suddenly makes sense: secret joy, adoration of an internal birth, of
an infant who knows many languages. From Mary of Nazareth to the
Marquise von O., their resistances oppose a natural and biological reason
to the mystery: how could I possibly conceive without a man? They still
don't believe in themselves. The bristling of reason has its own reasons:
as G. says, the resistances are bridges that eventually serve the inner
voice with greater clarity.
I don't think Christmas ever held a similar pregnancy for me, even during
the religious phase of my adolescence; I used to view it as an external
event, deriving from an objective religion. Now it is completely absorbed
by my own experiences.
Waiting as the ability to receive, passivity as quivering expansion, as
growth.

DECEMBER 25

I couldn't accept an invitation for Christmas lunch just to avoid being
alone. I do some yoga. I turn my attention inward.
Black, dense darkness that rises in waves from the scooped-out depth.
There are no images—if I imagine a human figure, it is swallowed up.
Again and again I return to the deep black cavity, every time my attention
flees and tries to wander elsewhere. The blackness continues all the way
to the earth.
I feel the weight of my heart without interruption and I let it drop again
and again. It sinks, descends, loses itself in the almost palpable darkness,
a thick, heavy substance. Absolute blackness of the cauldron in which I

am settled. Neither hope nor past. Not emotions, not feelings, not projections. Only downward toward the depths.

To recover I listen to *La Traviata*. I cry a lot, especially in the last act. I must have gone years without crying; now I have all these tears to shed. They untie knots, they reclaim the past.

La Traviata seen for the first time in a theater, I was maybe ten years old. I had stood in line in the street with my grandmother and other women, waiting for them to open the doors for the balcony, a separate entrance from the orchestra and boxes. Then a race up the stairs to grab seats, and more waiting. I already knew snatches of the opera, I heard my grandmother singing them and I heard them on the radio. But seeing the whole thing, following the plot! On the stage I recognized my own situation and its future. Violetta—I wanted to be like her, always free, without marriage or children. Like her I wanted a great love, without thinking about how it would turn out. Like her I felt alone in the world, without any support. Like her I was inclined, in the name of a father greater than my playful and absent papa—a father as strong as ideas, books, culture—to give up everything in favor of a pure, innocent young girl, the girl I myself was supposed to become. This double identity exerted a strong pull on me; alongside purity, I also wanted to go astray. At the price of destroying herself, Violetta was a rebel against a conformism that was suffocating me as well, in that small provincial city. And love and freedom were incompatible.

After the crushes of elementary school, the three years of middle school brought a halt to romances for me. It was a period of intensified female socializing: we created a little theater in a garage, for an audience of parents and neighborhood kids; outings, snacks, afternoons of doing homework together; we learned to dance among ourselves, at separate birthday parties.

Mixed socializing resumed in high school: slow and hesitant approaches, with great difficulty. We would start up conversations during the break, we would walk a little way together after school, study together occasionally, under family supervision. Everything was forbidden, even a passeggiata, which that provincial city's speedy gossip network would broadcast the very same evening.
The only outlet was a Catholic organization, which provided an opportunity to go to the mountains in mixed groups, to sing, eat, and live communally in the outdoors. A sort of problematic religiosity prevailed, with

participation in the liturgy and the opportunity for group discussions, for
mysticism and contemplation, all paths rejected by the conventional religion of adults. At long last, this was life, with room for flirting, new
acquaintances from other cities, the adventure of long outings staying
overnight in hostels. At the end of the vacation, we returned to our viscid
routine, which offered no way out, to the narrow-minded and conservative atmosphere of the small city. It was characterized by a dreadful cultural poverty, which motivated us to react by delving further and further
into the world of arts and letters: intense studying, intense reading, intense looking at painting and architecture, not just textbooks; hunger for
exhibits, concerts, new and different ideas. My best friend and I discussed
it for hours: the ideal would be to run away and live a bohemian life in
some great capital.

The atmosphere favored unhappy romances. I fell in love in turn, one
year each, with two guys who impressed me as rebels: one resembled
James Dean and behaved in a slightly crazy, wild, transgressive manner;
he dressed badly, answered insolently, conducted seances. The other was
a quiet type, thoughtful; he played the guitar; at parties he appeared and
disappeared with a mournful air. Walking up and down the main street
every evening at seven o'clock, arm-in-arm with a girlfriend, I managed
to catch a glimpse of him, to exchange greetings as we commented on the
window of the only record store. We looked at each other with an understanding superior to the world of the passeggiata, which we both disdained, participating in it with a detached manner and an empty gaze.
The passeggiata was important for trading news and gossip, exchanging
looks, putting on displays. The older boys arrived from the bars, havens of
the male clan, off-limits to and feared by us young women, who already
found it hard to walk by them, because of the implacable judgment of the
male stares.
My boyfriend appeared alone or with others, always disdainful and sad.
He let me know that he reciprocated my feelings; we went to see exhibits
together and to listen to music. But I also understood that our love would
remain unhappy.
In school there were interminable discussions with our classmates about
the differences between men and women and about vague notions of free
love. Some boys went to the only whorehouse in town and marked their
visits by notching their wooden desks. Those who couldn't afford it suffered in silence. They all talked about it at great length and explained to
us how cool the prostitutes, who had figured it all out, were—unlike us
girls, who created so many fantasies and were waiting for the great love.
These were the teenage years. We smoked in secret, drank all sorts of

liquor, talked endlessly about literature and music. I spent afternoons listening to two classmates who played the sax and the clarinet, imitating Charlie Parker. We read Sartre, Camus, Pavese, whom we loved in addition to everything else for his alienation from the existing world, proven by his suicide.

I kept a diary that alternated the record of my religious crises with that of my romances: "Today I believe in God but not in Christ"; "I saw P. on the main street and he crossed over to talk to me. He gave me a big smile. F. on the other hand was especially pale and barely greeted me"; "I think I've grasped the meaning of the figure of Christ; the meaning of Mary eludes me totally." Ultimately the study of Kant resolved one of the two problems drastically, providing the stimulus for an act of rebellion: I decided I was agnostic and I left the Church.

In the third year of high school, there was a major new development: I took part in a cultural circle that aimed at uniting workers, peasants, and students. No peasants showed up; there were some very young workers and others who were not so young, who had been in the Resistance as kids and recounted their adventures to us, enjoying enormous prestige in our eyes. All this meant going out at night, going to taverns, singing political songs and old Piedmontese songs; it generated endless family squabbles. We also went to see old partisans who lived in the country. They cooked hare, told captivating stories, which we stayed late into the night to hear, drinking wine. They were communists, but not in the sense of the bureaucratic party; it was the Red tradition, which spoke of subversion, of hidden arms and reconquest, but also of jokes, pranks, and above all of nonresignation after the Liberation. There was a story going around about the partisan Rocca, who barricaded himself on a hillside for five days before the Communist leaders convinced him to come down; a story, like others, told in hushed tones. We understood that there were still weapons, somewhere. All this made some of us ready for anything in the years to come. There were no role models, we didn't know how to act, between the prohibitions and the innovations. There was just the desire to fling the entire old world into the sea.

At the end of high school—it was the beginning of the sixties—international exchange programs provided an opportunity for escape. My best friend and I left for a year in the United States, in two different cities, managing to spend a few days together in New York. I attended an American high school; I had a regular boyfriend, a legendary baseball player, who had a sports car he had bought by selling newspapers for years and years, who talked about getting married. But most of all, I had a family, with par-

ents and two sisters. Mom, my American mother, was tall and lively, she liked to dance and to entertain friends. Very religious, very sociable. Careful not to stifle anyone in the family, but ready to help. She told me about having had various relationships with men, but then of having ultimately found a true harmony with her husband, a placid man who joked easily. They went out often, alone and with other couples, they took trips, they enjoyed life. To me they seemed limited, provincial, backward. I was fond of them, but I couldn't follow through on that affection, wrapped up as I was in my furies of rebellion. In order not to betray those furies while in the United States, I took a Russian course taught, unfortunately, by an aristocrat who regularly cursed the Revolution since it had forced her family to flee. Dad made fun of me for my fierce anticlericalism and suggested that I write to the Pope announcing that I was abandoning Catholicism: "Dear Pope, I quit."
Memory of another Christmas, with a tree and gifts, amid Christmas carols and an enormous turkey, which lasted for days on end.

DECEMBER 28

I finished the interviews on '68. We met in Paris to tie up all the loose ends. It's clear that the international book can't be a history of subjectivity; there is insufficient time to do the comparisons and the analyses, given the deadlines imposed by the publishers who have financed us; there is insufficient money for meeting together. It will be a narrative of some of the paths.
I will have to work alone on memory, and perhaps not for the purpose of producing a history. Or rather, not for the purpose of producing a history book.

I want to attempt a reading of these life stories, including my own. Take up the same thread from the other end, talk about what I've seen in the mirrors held up by those I've interviewed.

2

Choosing to be Orphans

Beginnings

At the roots of our memory, in dozens of life histories, I find a rupture. Our identity is constructed on contradictions. Even those stories that emphasize the continuity of their own lives extract from the autobiographical material—as far as the formative years are concerned—recurring themes of division, of difference, of contrast.

The subject matter of these narratives is the Italy of the post–World War II period, the years of our childhood and adolescence. A country divided by twenty years of Fascism and by a civil war that cut across families, leaving deep furrows. The civil war continued in a cold war pitting Socialists against Communists against Catholics, right against left, and still divides the left on the question of the relationship between communism and democracy, on the role of the Soviet Union in the defense of liberty.

The accounts speak of social injustices, which are more noticeable as a result of greater mobility. The rapid rise in fortune of some strata highlights the deprivations of many, and waves of immigrants exacerbate tensions and domestic racism. Conflicts emerge based on class, on regions and neighborhoods, on politics and religion; north against south, old immigrants against new, rich against poor, old money and new money; highbrow and lowbrow, Italian language and local dialect.

In the stories, social differences are interwoven with conflicts ingrained in families, in friendships, in individuals. Marriages reflect the divergences between people of different cultures and strata: children's recollections bear traces of rancors going back to earliest childhood, proving that one is never too young to be called on to take sides.

It's not just a matter of translating general contradictions into the private sphere. The opposite is also true: disagreements arise in interpersonal relationships and are then expanded on a larger scale. The masculine/feminine polarity, experienced through parental figures, refers to other social processes and to more extensive polemics; women, who just won the right to vote (in 1945) and are increasing their presence in the work force, find themselves on the brink of vast social, economic, and psychological changes.

Memory has recorded the repercussions: the suffering due to inequalities, frustrations endured or witnessed. But not only that. For memory speaks from today. It speaks from the point of view of a constructed identity, a political identity in the old sense of the term: a citizenship conferred and not easily canceled; a shared identity, participation in the creation of one's own life and in the invention of a culture.

It is this identity that tries to create for itself a memory and that must reinterpret the past. All those who contributed to the formation of the new culture may not have suffered the social inequalities and the individual traumas of the preceding years in the same way. And, on the other hand, many experienced the contradictions and their aftermath—the economic boom, the new youth market, the accentuation and shifting of the man/woman difference—without then becoming card-carrying citizens of the new society.

In other words, there is no causal relationship between socioeconomic circumstances and the new subjectivity. How many became adherents and proponents of the subjective upturn, compared to the overall number of their contemporaries? How many individuals, from the generations born between the end of the 1930s and the beginning of the 1950s, had a 1968?

Even if it isn't feasible to quantify a percentage, it is possible to attempt to evaluate a difference. The hypothesis is that the protagonists of this cultural transformation—each in his or her own way—bear its traces on the level of memory, even if the operation is still in progress and in certain cases appears interrupted.

Memory narrates with the vivid tones of actual experience. But what interests me is neither the liveliness of the accounts nor their faithfulness to reality, both of which would make these stories a secondary source for a good social history of Italy after 1945. Rather, what attracts me is memory's insistence on creating a history of itself, which is much less and perhaps somewhat more than a social history.

The undertaking is difficult because it quickly bumps into a paradox, already experienced in the moments when a new identity glimmered as a possibility. To become history, this subjectivity must assert itself as antihistorical. It must nullify, distance, destroy. And even where it finds continuity—with revolts of the past—it must manifest that as discontinuity.

The discussion of one's own roots seeks to supply the context surrounding a political birth. The interpretation of the link between roots and context is delicate. The recollection of conflicts acquires meaning if we understand it not as the cause of that birth but as an obstacle that, in order to be overcome or eliminated, demands a leap beyond "two completely different worlds."

Eliana Minicozzi (born 1942, Rome):
Around the age of eleven my father began to work as a baker's helper and then gradually he learned the welder's trade. After 1943 he and my grandfather had a machine-shop where they made three-pronged nails for the Resistance. These were steel nails that they threw to blow out tires, and they made them in a forge that heated the metal, I remember, as a child. I also remember May Days with trucks full of people, including us, with red carnations. I remember my grandparents returning from political rallies with their heads busted.
And your mother?
My mother, that's a totally different experience, a very bourgeois family originally, Sicilian, economic and family disasters. She liked the theater, reading, music, she was very Catholic. Up to the age of thirteen I tried to be sort of like my mother—major traumas because I went to school with the nuns, where they took me off the honor roll, they didn't promote me in piano, and they told me, "The devil is going to get you because your father is a Communist." Around thirteen I shifted toward my father, that is, I said, I remember, to the Sacred Heart, "I don't know if you agree or not, but I prefer to love humanity than to love you." I began to hand out the Communist paper *Unità*, to present myself as a political girl.

Laura Derossi (born 1946, Turin):
I come from a bourgeois family, a wealthy family. My father was a building contractor and also had a small metalwork business, but he wasn't a reactionary, he voted Liberal. I went to school with the Dominican nuns, elementary school, middle school, and classical high school, and I associated with the best Turin families, dances, parties. But an environment that was fundamental to my development was the family of my building custodian, Tosca, who made tortellini that were

out of this world, treated me kindly, protected me. I lived in the courtyard with the little boys from the neighborhood, I was a tomboy. I
waited to go home until my father returned, because he didn't object
like the others: "Laura shouldn't go in the courtyard, what's Laura
doing all day at Tosca's"—my mother felt like she was to blame—
"She's going to end up on the streets." And in fact, then . . .

Romano Madera (born 1948, Varese):

I experienced two different worlds. One was the industrial world, the
new world, which for someone else would have been normal, for me it
wasn't, because every summer we spent two and a half months in
Calabria, with my grandparents. And there it really was another world.
Trips that lasted for days, because the world ended at Metaponto and
you had to take the choo-choo, the steam train, to get to that other
world of Cariati. Then from Cariati, to go the remaining eleven kilometers, five to Torretta and six to the village, Crucoli, it took another half
day. Another world: the people, but also the things. No one had running water in their homes, we went to get it from the fountain, which
was a kilometer and a half away. My grandfather came on horseback,
because there was only one bus at dawn and one at sunset. The mules,
the herds, a vast daily procession of goats, sheep. A language I understood poorly: in my house—brothers and sisters born in Rome, Vene-
tian mother, Calabrese father—we weren't accustomed to utter even a
word in dialect, because basically the others wouldn't have understood and that would have been that! I never understood the Lombard
dialect very well, and I never learned pure Calabrese.

Marco Revelli (born 1947, Cuneo):

My first march was a procession, and I went on it when the Madonna
of Fatima came. I remember that she set down in Cuneo just under the
helicopter, and she set down in the main square—there were probably
thirty thousand people, the first big crowd I ever saw. I had gone to see
the helicopter and to be with my friends. All these people falling to
their knees, women starting to cry, struck me tremendously. It was a
sight that really impressed me, and then we had this big procession
with torches. I was very proud of going on a march with my friends for
the first time, a first experience of this kind. Then I went home but it
wasn't like this triumph got a similar reception from my parents. My
father was a Socialist, a partisan commander, my mother went with
me to the square and pointed out to me how ugly the cops were in their
military uniforms.

Ambiguity Toward Fathers

The continuity/discontinuity link plays itself out primarily in the ambivalent quality of the paternal figure. Many fathers are presented as "liberals" in the sense that they aspired to ideals of liberalism defined by their children as "nineteenth-century": tolerance, belief in freedom, in private enterprise, in work, in culture. The ambivalence isn't only in the children's feelings; the fathers themselves are ambiguous parental figures, affectionate and absent, authoritarian and weak, opponents of clericalism in their families and perhaps in their voting habits, but respectful of conventions, supporters of a religious upbringing that will sometimes cause conflicts with their children.

And yet these fathers furnish the imagination with some sparks of a possible rebellion. Taking the teachings of the fathers' liberal side literally, the children will be able to insist on carrying the aspiration for liberty and justice to its extreme. Ten or twenty years later, the children can accuse the fathers of not being sufficiently consistent; they can expect disapproval, but also a secret satisfaction on the part of the fathers regarding these children who were braver than they themselves; every once in a while a father will even undergo a "conversion":

Romano Madera:
At the end of the war the partisans hunted my father as a collaborator. On the other side the Fascists were looking for him for the opposite reason. In reality, he was hiding out. They put him on the purge lists, they tried him and absolved him. At first he voted Liberal, but gradually he shifted, under the influence of his relationship with his kids as well. His real god was culture—two degrees and certification as an elementary school principal—the Liberal Party had been the party of Croce, that was crucial. Then he moved quickly to the left; first the PSDI (Italian Social-Democratic Party) during the period of unification; then in the split he stayed with the PSI (Italian Socialist Party); ultimately he became mayor of the Social-communist junta!

These fathers provided the values that nourished certain of their children's attitudes, that sustained them throughout certain periods. Carrying on the idea of honor handed down by a father, a liberal Neapolitan lawyer, will facilitate the transition to communism, learned from a high school classmate (Momo, born 1951, Naples). That transition, the subject of heated discussions with his father, will lead to a profound break and only much later to a reconciliation and to the recognition of an early ambivalence: honor mixed with that nineteenth-century cynical opportunism we both "have in our blood" (Momo).

Parental figures on the left, militant Catholics, anti-Fascists, progressives don't escape this ambivalence. The culture that the new generation wants to establish demands a nonlinear emancipation, for it must be a double emancipation, from society and from the family. A Communist father is delighted for his daughter to preach free love, but can't stand for her to practice it (Minicozzi). The figure of the anti-Fascist father, an intellectual, member of the Partito d'Azione (Action Party), elicits in the son a reaction of excessive severity, almost a rigidity, in order to avoid yielding to overly simple suggestions of continuity (Luigi Bobbio, born 1944, Turin). In these cases the contradictions are no less strong nor the outcomes less obscure on the personal level.

The new culture is one of opposition. When it succeeds, it's dialectical: in its discontinuity with respect to the liberal father it seeks a continuity of values; in its continuity with the proletarian tradition it recognizes a lack of consistency on the level dearest to it, the level of identity.

Franco Russo (born 1945, Benevento):
I came from a working class family, my father was a carpenter and my mother was a building custodian, in other words the sum total of working-class nobility. My father has always been a Socialist, and he used to take me to political rallies, but the party newspaper, *Avanti!*, had to be kept hidden. My father got no help from his political party in making his proletarian status an element of his social identity, there was a continual masking of this identity. There's always been a shadowy area in which we lived our home life.

A patrimony of struggle that includes models of deference, acquiescence, imitation, and concealment posits an internal conflict. On this question no difference appears to exist among the three age groups that make up the political generation we are discussing. There is the central group, the largest, which experienced 1967–68 at the university, as students; there are those who were already working but who nonetheless were involved more or less radically; and there is the younger group, who were in middle or high school and came to be called the *medi*.

Looking at the birth dates, it is striking that they are only partially determinative of affiliation with one of the three groups. Nineteen forty-two could be the birth date of someone who already had a college degree and a job in 1968, but also of someone who was still a college student. The actual situation depends on the faculty, on social and geographic background, on the personal circumstances of each individual.

Biological age is more determinative of affiliation for the third group; those born after 1950 experienced the university students' movement, but in their own schools. Thus, in general, the relationship with their families is different, but in certain instances the attitude toward rebellion is also different. There is a sense of emulation, of eagerness to make the revolt their own and to make a unique contribution.

The difference is not in their attitudes toward biological fathers. I sense the same tones in the just-quoted narrative of Franco Russo and in that of Marino Sinibaldi, who were born ten years apart. Marino comments without sarcasm on the attitude of his father, who writes to a government minister in order to save his son when he's suspended from school, or on his mother's disgust at his long hair. He simply distances himself.

Marino Sinibaldi (born 1954, Rome):
My mother is a housewife, Catholic, you could call her a militant Christian Democrat. My father was a tram-driver, a union man, but mainly Christian Democrat in his last years. They met in the parish. I was born in a neighborhood with a strong anarchist and socialist tradition, my grandfather was a kiln-worker, and in the square the anarchist daily *Umanità Nuova* was always posted in addition to *Unità*. But I went to the Mamiani high school, and therein lies a pathetic family tale. My grandmother did laundry for the rich people in the Prati neighborhood and my mother told me, when I was already big, that when she was little she used to go with my grandmother to pick up and deliver the laundry, and she would go by the Mamiani school and see all these beautiful kids with their cars. And she really went to a lot of trouble so that I could go to the Mamiani, since ordinarily because of the district I would have gone to another high school. When she revealed this to me, of course it radicalized my hatred for this school.

The difference is that the third age group has older siblings. Sometimes this will produce a mixture of adoration and envy, efforts to live up to the inherited revolt, a push toward radicalism. For them, even more than for the central group, there is only one possible attitude with respect to the equivocal nature of the father as a symbolic figure: discontinuity.

Independently of biological data, of age, and of flesh-and-blood fathers, some life histories make the symbolic plane and the real plane converge, almost coincide. On this point the various age groups concur, finding a peer group unity. Some personalities lend themselves to this role better than others, even when the autobiographical material contains elements that might tend toward ambiguity:

Guido Viale (born 1943, Tokyo):
I was orphaned by my father at eleven, and by my mother at twenty-one. Politically, my father had liberal ideas.

The prevailing message, which becomes a culture and the criterion for identification, is the status as orphan, summed up in one terse statement that suggests the entire context of the life history: "I never had any maestros" (Viale).

At the end of the sixties orphanhood will become a slogan, derisory and profane.

Fiorella Farinelli (born 1943, Viareggio):
The best poster on the walls of my faculty, I remember it really distinctly, out of all the posters there: "I want to be an orphan." I shared that feeling, I took a picture of it, I brought the poster home, it was the one I liked best of all: "I want to be an orphan."

This tone of negation, of rejection, of repudiation, puts its stamp on the language. It is the divergent method of expressing the same substance that forms the basis for this world view. "Me, I don't have a father," Mario Dalmaviva (born 1940, Milan) responds to a direct question, choosing this from all the possible ways of saying the same thing.

Sometimes, instead, it is hyperbole, a humorous tone, that serves to create distance. Franco Aprà (born 1945, Venice), Piedmontese father and Abruzzese mother, from a family that had to relocate often because of the father's work (at the Bank of Italy), glorifies these facts with irony: "I don't have a real fatherland, I have mixed blood."

Language shapes biographical events within an interpretation of the world and of history. Life experience is suddenly transported into a public sphere with literary value.

Roberto Dionigi (born 1941, Pesaro):
The extremes: petty bourgeois, two schoolteachers, one of physical
education, one of humanities. They live on what they earn, nothing
else, my paternal grandfather was a tavern-keeper, the other one was
a marshal in the carabinieri in Sicily.
Lots of beatings, intense Fascist pedagogy.
I don't have anything in my house, no memorabilia, nothing comes
from my family. The only thing is a set of the great foreign authors
published by UTET, I think it was a wedding present my mother got.
Decisive experience: I encountered Baudelaire for the first time, at
seventeen.

The distancing between cultural birth and family and social origins is clear, as if we were aliens thrust into this world and searching
for others like ourselves. Each one takes his or her own status literally, in a motion that will be unique to this culture, a founding act
that is also an awareness of the negative, without illusions or regrets.
Not without sadness, as those who many years later admit to having
felt the "desire for a maestro to guide me" will observe: "a basic element, that everybody in the culture of my generation missed out on,
especially the women" (Paola Di Cori, born 1946, Buenos Aires). But
that is just the point, this is in hindsight. In the formative moments of
the new cultural attitude, following a period of vague and impatient
waiting, an estrangement from the entire past, the impossibility of
identifying with any part of it had to take precedence.

Fiorella Farinelli quotes a college classmate at the Normal School
at Pisa who expressed the feelings of many in that generation: "You
can't just stand around doing nothing but studying just to become a
university assistant and be stuck there. You've got to do something
else with your life!"

A beacon for that confused yearning did appear: the image of the
Resistance. But the inspiration the official memory of the Resistance
provided for this nascent obliterating state of mind was aptly described in the early sixties. I remember agreeing passionately with
the opinion expressed in the journal *Quaderni Piacentini*, a forum
for Marxist ideas on economics and politics, culture, and society
published by young intellectuals in the provincial town of Piacenza:

NO. NO. NO. We don't want the dead of the Resistance to be "honored"
with monuments "to the fallen of all wars" dedicated by the bishop,
prefect, president of the tribunal, district commander, commissioners,
lieutenants and superintendents. Better silence.

The underlying problem is that to activate a true continuity, appropriate for the times, one has to go through a discontinuity. The story of Federico De Luca Comandini (born 1952, Rome) is emblematic. "The tradition in my mother's family was democratic-radical: Jacobins, then Risorgimento, Garibaldians, then Republicans, then Action Party." A family that summarizes rebellion at its best. On his father's side, "a less solidified tradition time-wise, but he was in the Resistance: my father and mother met in the Resistance." But the story of Federico as a child is far removed from this political heritage; he paints himself as bent on chasing philosophical fantasies and girls; nothing else interested him. It will take an unusual situation, the occupation and closure of his high school, for him to discover himself and his calling and to acknowledge an emotional continuity: "My wife and I met at the occupation of the Mamiani high school."

This tone is unusual among my stories: the reconciled calmness, the certainty of continuity with himself and with '68, as well as with the affective tradition: "aside from the obfuscation of the years 1969–71—more than obfuscation it was a shift of energy—I've never lost touch with my experience of '68." My interpretation is that the sense of continuity *from* '68 is closely connected to the perception of the discontinuity *of* '68 with respect to prior (and subsequent) history. Federico's story is also the one that most explicitly comprehends '68 as a radical departure:

> We're not talking about '68 or '88, we're talking about an epochal change that is in progress and that will take generations. A psychological structure doesn't change in two months or two years.

We are encountering the heart of this autobiographical memory, its *raison d'être*—the connection between the individual and the collective. The language divides between past and present: "It was an independence movement based on individual motivations," says today's reflection. Recollection translates: "As we used to say then, 'Starting from a concrete situation,' that is, I can start from my own experience." Not only does the importance of the individual, the shift from external to internal, emerge; there is another epoch-making reversal: from the masculine to the feminine, from a limited logos, deprived of its natural warmth, to the "clarity of feelings."

> The element that socialized me in '68 was its emotional impact. 'Sixty-eight validated the sentimental, imaginative factors that are the feminine aspects of our culture, psychologically speaking. In opposition to

a psychological structure basically oriented toward male values, it liberated psychological qualities that were undervalued—the imagination in power—affective values, traditionally ascribed to women.

Rejection of the Mother

It is not by chance, then, that in our memory the antihistorical attitude appears particularly accentuated with respect to the mother figure. Is it perhaps an indication that the most energetic distancing had to occur precisely at that point, in the relationship with the individual's own internal image of the feminine and with the social role of women? At first the fruits of such a breach are not visible. Youth belongs to the father; rebellion pursues the myth of the young hero, at times semi-adolescent, at times androgynous, but more boy than girl, although softened by thoughtfulness and indignation—like the protagonist of the film *Della conoscenza*, produced by the Roman student movement in 1969 and directed by a woman, Alessandra Bocchetti.

A young man, blond and thoughtful, crosses the city, from the halls of the occupied university to the demonstrations in the center of town. Smoke-filled assemblies of students in jackets and ties alternate with images of liberation struggles in Asia and Africa, battles with the police at the architecture faculty alternate with images of napalmed children. And then the squalid outskirts of Rome, students throwing books out the window, the black ghettoes of the United States. A desire for freedom and a desire to transform completely the relationship with knowledge pass over the whole world. The young hero who ties all this together is neither ingenuous nor ironic; if anything, he resembles the alienated characters who ambled through the films of the French *nouvelle vague.* His image is far removed from the traditional image of virility; his face is not coarsened by the professional revolutionary's beard; his gaze is detached, his demeanor calm. A new man, who has appropriated some of the characteristics of femininity? or who, antedating sexual differentiation, appears as androgynous, double, indifferent?

This will constitute one of the thorny problems of the sixties and the seventies—the relationship between '68 and the women's movement, between political liberation and emotional and sexual liberation. But in the beginning the problem manifests itself in the form of difficulty in accepting the known feminine, in talking about the mother and about the relationship with her.

The mother goes unmentioned, barely touched on, in these stories, even under the pressure of direct questions. Her figure hides a complex issue, which will appear only with the development of the life history, a preliminary issue perhaps, linked to early childhood, about which there is much reticence: "I don't know whether I had a happy or unhappy childhood" (Bobbio), and which definitely arrives late, in the symptoms of the second half of life or in the perception of maturity.

Our generation's formative period is especially long, and not only because of our tardiness in getting established professionally. The cultural work required is immense, the psychological work risky and delicate. Neither the former nor the latter always succeeds. Processes that have accelerated in recent decades require readjustment and re-elaboration: there is a shift away from the notion of work as the fundamental ethic of life and of education as the vehicle for social mobility and indicator of culture, toward the separation between work-related ability and identity, toward the addition of other elements as bases for self-esteem (mobility, entertainment), toward the growing gap between degree and occupation, between upbringing and spiritual perfection. We must add to all this the difficulty of conceptualizing the feminine pole of one's own personality, updating one's evaluation of it.

Thus it is only subsequent to the phase characterized by revolt that one can come to terms with the inner mother.

Pedro Humbert (born 1948, Cremona):
I internalized my father figure a lot and only later, in a mature phase, did I begin to discover the troublesome aspects of this paternal figure and, by contrast, the strong aspects of my mother's personality, which I had experienced in a positive fashion, but as a secondary figure. During the phase of my intellectual and political maturation, my mother was more important than my father. She was more open to change: the process of change was more profound in her, more radical compared to the life she led, and in my father it was more superficial.

The individual process accompanies historical trends regarding the concept and image of the feminine in the fifties and sixties. For that period, the distancing appears in retrospect as not so much a conscious act of subjectivity as an obscure impulsive reflex, almost a spontaneous withdrawal, an unmeditated repulsion, out of nausea, disgust, aversion. The rejection is violent primarily in the women's stories, which sketch a conflict rather divergent from the ambivalences of the relationship with the father figure. Not wanting to be like one's mother is a recurrent reference in the women's stories, in some cases reinforced by the mother herself (albeit in an almost unwitting manner, by "symptoms of rebellion, not a conscious effort," Mariella Tagliero, born 1945, Luserna S. Giovanni), in other cases acted out against the mother:

Fiorella Farinelli:
I knew that in my life I wanted to be everything except what my mother was, that's it. This was absolutely clear to me. And so I misbehaved quite a bit. I smoked in secret, I smoked at parties, I always went out dancing, even when my mom didn't want me to. I wanted to go out at night, and then, okay, in truth the big sin was love.

Maria Teresa Fenoglio (born 1947, Genoa):
My mother was southern in every respect. She bore the southern culture of magical influence, the evil eye. It was impossible for me to identify with such a threatening maternal figure, tied to the great power of the benevolent and malevolent mother. Another maternal trait, something my mother really had, was a delight in exhibitionism, lacquered red nails, tight skirts, make-up. In my adolescence, when I tried to imitate her, the result was a huge sense of depression, because I judged myself. I couldn't like myself in that guise, because from the standpoint of ideal choices I sided with my father—Social Democrat and then Socialist, one of the few commanders of the non-Communist Garibaldi unit: democratic ideas, conviction of being superior to others, material things don't count for us. The rift with my father came about then with my choice of sexual freedom.

The profound transformations in the fifties and sixties that beset the status of women—protagonists of the new consumerism, of changes in the care of one's body, of new everyday behaviors—were also transformations in the internal condition. There had always been exceptions to the separation and the hierarchy of masculine and feminine understood in the traditional sense, but perhaps they were becoming more numerous, more widespread, more disruptive. A certain confusion, a hesitation about designated roles appears in the narratives.

Maria Nadotti (born 1949, Turin) tells of an even-tempered father who worked at his job as manager of a company, not exhibiting any pronounced attitudes, in contrast with the active militancy of her mother in the Fascist Party in the fifties and sixties.

We breathed two airs: the feminine was political, and the masculine was professionalism, work, productive labor. And the feminine tendency was frustrated because my mother was the stay-at-home wife of a professional man in this sleepy town of Biella.

Inversions and displacements don't remove the sense of disquiet toward the feminine, hard to find, to appropriate, to understand: "I continued for years to think that the masculine figure in my house was my mother, not my father." The feminine comes to be chosen because it is disguised as masculine: this is the secret of success of figures like the vamp, the *femme fatale,* the sexually liberated, aggressive, "modern" woman.

The models provided by known women offer extreme cues for rebellion, not ambiguous ones like those of the fathers. If they are strong, they are relentlessly strong, as if rigidified by a gigantesque effort, overly serious, lacking humorous flashes, while this generation aspires to a culture that appropriates the dimension of play, of the student prank, capable of later metamorphosing from its humorous origins into critique of the status quo.

Vittorio Dini (born 1945, Naples):
Basically my mother was the real head of the family, the more rational one compared to my father, who sometimes used to play practical jokes. Once he brought home a Sardinian donkey and this was considered a major sin because it was a waste of money, an extravagance.
It was a bit extravagant. . . .
Well, yeah, a bit, but all in all it was justified by the emptiness in which he usually lived, partly of necessity. But he was a nice person.

Or else the mothers appear as subordinated, subjugated, silent. They promise nothing, at least in the phase of identification with the Robin Hoods of the weak and rejection of one's own weakness. Throughout this period the feminine functions secretly, like a coiled spring, against injustice; but it is laden with conflicts, which become operative with other women, including one's own mother.

Laura Derossi:
I discovered my mother's existence a few years ago.
She was a person who never reacted, wasn't prone to violent outbursts, strong reactions, fallings-out, but quietly, secretly, she always

maintained her forms of independence. She seemed like a weak person, whom I always rejected, and whose actual strength—which in reality was immense, because she left her mark on my upbringing from behind the scenes—I didn't discover until recently.

The weak mother was something that had to be avenged: this is something I think I've always carried with me, that I had to avenge my mother in some fashion.

The difficulty of contemplating the feminine is, in reality, nothing more than the inability to accept oneself, the uniqueness of being an individual. Because the feminine must compare itself with its historical versions which, however limited, have depths to plumb and lessons to teach. Accepting the toughness of the mother-head-of-household or the apparent weakness of the housewife is a fortune we mustn't squander. Nor is it only a matter of a package of values now reaffirmed, such as feminine intelligence or intellectuality. No, the feminine is the uniqueness of each woman, her way of being herself (and perhaps the relationship with the other within himself, for each man).

But in the historical conditions of the fifties and sixties, this cultural transformation was taking place, especially for women, in opposition to other women, at the expense of their relationships with one another. Intellectual emancipation (doing well in school) could serve as the basis for a new freedom of behavior, but that necessitated an alliance with the father, symbolic or real. If real, it could provoke violent jealousies in other women, mothers, and sisters (Tagliero). It foreshadowed the cruel relationships that would be inaugurated in the course of another emancipation, the political emancipation of 1968.

From Justine to Griselda

3

JANUARY

Dinner with a new acquaintance. I said I was in analysis and he, "Me too, me too," but in another city. The usual conversation, *The Magic Mountain*, *Wilhelm Meister*, our shared Piedmontese culture, food, recollections from the sixties and seventies.
I recognize the pathways of seduction.

So, here we are right in the midst of it; rapidly picking up momentum, this romance asserts itself from minute to minute. The distractions are slight: as soon as I conclude an engagement, as soon as I leave a lunch or a meeting I rediscover the image of this man whom I can't call by name—almost as if it were something between me and myself—and I discover that during the brief absence the feeling has become stronger and more dominant. I was fascinated by our meeting three days ago: his light complexion and grey hair, his sometimes slightly effeminate gestures, his calm manner of talking and sudden smiles, his tall, strong stature. And his clothes: a red pullover, beautiful.

Talking with G. about falling in love, I say, "This damnable stuff," and he pretends to hear "annual stuff." One of the things I had explained to him as a symptom was my falling in love often, eliciting grief and shame, almost a recurrent nightmare; every time it seemed absurd, ill-advised, and directed at the wrong person.

The interviews on 1968 have left their traces. In some cases, we have become friends. Others reconsider, phone me, want to know what point the work has reached. I fear that in any event I will produce something inadequate.

For days I buried myself in documents regarding Turin 1968. They convey upheaval, but also the everyday repetitiousness of the struggle. High and low registers reflect different levels of culture, at times different levels of literacy. Bombastic expressions are attenuated by bad spelling; the poor quality of the mimeographing makes the subtlety of certain reflections more moving. I also read a lot of newspapers, looked at the photos, where my interviewees appear splendid, young, decisive. Everything seems very remote, archaic, securely ensconced in these archives, whence my research resuscitates the image like a holograph. Only an archive provides this kind of emotion, not the memory.

Convocation of the academic year. The rector, carrying his staff and wearing his ermine cape, the fur a bit worn. "Seventeen years," he said, "since this ceremony was interrupted by momentous events," the fateful academic year 1967–68.

I read X's books, I saw him again. He spends half the week here, the rest of the time in another city with his family. He travels continually, from meeting to presentation to conference. As I used to do not long ago.

FEBRUARY

Another birthday. This year I had a party. The house seemed changed, with new spaces to welcome friends. X forgot to phone me, as he had promised, to wish me happy birthday.

I dreamed about a young hermaphrodite. My relationship with X also seemed hermaphroditic to me, as if between two beings too much alike, until we made love. And then his almost specialistic way of doing it became apparent, genital, concentrated. Not much attention to the relationship between whole bodies. Even the words used were terms that referred to a sexual sphere without emotions. This is the difference between us. "I see growing in you a love . . . of difference," G. comments.

Now I suddenly find myself relegated to the role of lover, who takes second place to family, work, official responsibilities. Zaira, my friend-sister, observes, "these days the situation of a lover isn't so bad. And then it's such a big change for you."

Nor does G. agree that the situation is the disaster I think it is. "Dis-aster," he says, alluding to my models of stellar distances in relationships, which this throws into confusion. The image of myself as reserved, aloof, distant—I would like to demolish it little by little, even if it seems like my only defense.

I am torn between the desire to see him and acceptance of the waiting. He has made himself unattainable, with the seducer's technique: disappearing right after making love. G. exhibits complete empathy when I remind him of the effect of this technique as described by Kierkegaard. In the past I too had made use of similar cruel modes of behavior. Now it appears uncivilized to me, almost as if we were living in a primitive state. I feel a need for civility—democracy—even in love.

Dream: I am wading in the water and at a certain point I notice with disgust the algae under my feet. In addition, threatening waves are breaking, the water is yellow, the storm is growing, there is no longer any help or any escape.
Stuck here waiting for a phone call.

The past months of solitude and abstinence, almost like a reconquest of virginity, definitely a reconquest of modesty and a new devotion. My body responds to his—I feel the cold less. I would like to communicate to him the minutia of my everyday life, that today I bought myself two pairs of high heels, on sale.
After many years, I take up listening to a lot of music again.

X appears at intervals. Passionate, "violently seductive" love affairs, G. observes seeing the consequences. Then X disappears for long periods, even as long as eleven days. Perhaps for this reason I count everything: how many days since I washed my hair and until I can wash it again, how many days between appointments with Dr. G., how many days until the beginning of the next month, which will, perhaps, be better than this one.

I am troubled by the thought of the women who share X with me: his mother, his wife, a sister. Once upon a time I disdained jealousy. I wonder whether I don't want him mainly in order to have one of them, the mother. But the whole thing bothers me, it seems immoral.
"You wanted to be the only one?" G. is imperturbable.
He seems to consider this throng of women normal. Instead it makes me very wary with regard to the man in a position of power. "But he does have some ideals," I protest, "a faith." It doesn't matter, it's useful to

doubt, G.'s face insists. How can I visualize X among the bullies? He is an avenging angel.

MARCH

We visit an exhibit X had told me about with some friends. Every room, every display case is like a sharp thorn. Now I understand the fable of the mermaid who exchanged her tail for a woman's legs. The man didn't love her, although he wanted her with him always, and at every step the mermaid felt an acute pain in her legs.
That's what it's like, like having an open wound. Of course everything passes through the wound: emotions, memories, attention to things previously neglected.

A great docility, that's what one of the cloistered nuns in Zavoli's old radio documentary counseled as, in their experience, the most important trait to have. In mine too.

X winces if I try to tell him I love him. "I prefer that you don't love me, that way we can be fond of each other." But he gets irked when I respond: "Maybe this trial had to happen to me." He says he has enough of violence and grief, and that he would like a tranquil relationship with me. Right, so I should have to give up expressing my passion and my hurt?

Always attached to the phone, like Claretta Petacci, who dragged it with her from the bath to the couch to the bed.

Image from this morning: I was reading and at a certain point my obsession with phoning X diminished. I visualized extricating myself from a large spiderweb, I had shaken myself free of it and was pushing it away with my feet the way you do when you're taking off your socks or boots. I tossed it away reduced to shreds, and once again it came up to my neck, and once again I pushed it down to my feet and freed myself from it, in a continual transition.

I think a year of analysis has predisposed me to this love affair and that G. has encouraged me. I tell him that, and he gets a bit impatient:
"But hadn't this ever happened to you before? an unhappy love affair?"
Well no, it hadn't happened to me since I was seventeen, in the foolish

fifties. In the subsequent twenty years I fell out of love quickly if someone didn't love me, it only took me a few days or weeks.

If I think of the vexation—a moment of allure followed quickly by irritation—it caused me to be the recipient of demands for love which I couldn't/wouldn't reciprocate. And my withdrawal increased the frantic insistence of the demand, as is now happening to me. Perhaps because of this reversal, I feel like someone who must undergo a trial. And also because I hope ultimately these tribulations will make sense.

Frequently the image comes to mind of Griselda, married off to the Marquis of Saluzzo, an unrepentant bachelor, who, in order to test her love, takes away her children pretending to kill them; he repudiates her and throws her out with only the clothes on her back, but later recalls her to have her prepare everything for his new marriage to a beautiful young girl. Eventually he reveals to her that the young girl is one of her two children, both healthy and flourishing; after thirteen years he declares to her his love ("above every other thing I love you"), honoring her and causing her to be honored.

In this phase religious tension and love for X appear together, mixed. But the man gets frightened—rightly—by a woman who erupts. Only a god could reciprocate all this emotion. Only the "u"? only the relationship with oneself.

X phoned that he's leaving. For two weeks I'm safe. What is all this? Slavery, misery, debasement. Ever the economics of robbery, even in love: to possess and be possessed at all costs, exclusively. I would like a respectable love, a couple's relationship less subjugated to passion.

Excessively elaborate, long, complicated dreams. G can barely manage to follow my detailed and pedantic summaries.

This love affair is a means of testing the relationship with the unconscious, in another one of its disguises. Juggler, swindler, buffoon, minstrel. Joker, jester, jerk—trickster. Hermes. It's also a recapitulation of adolescence: enchanted religiosity, intense friendships, unhappy romances. And then there's the trial: love without being loved, but without being rejected either. Wait without anything to wait for, accept one's own desire for the unattainable, one's own complicity in oppression. The distance between the other and myself can be experienced as the internal distance between outpost and resistance; exercise to perform every day: expanding the inner space with torment.

If it is a trial, it doesn't just go toward the past, but toward a future. However, the examination of the past, the sense of expiation by means of *con-trappasso*—Dantesque retribution—is an obligatory step. What I had theorized in the sixties comes back to haunt me.

I had done to others what X is doing to me, separating feelings from sexuality, insisting on a freedom and an availability that are always false—ways of escaping from the relationship with oneself in order to be like Don Giovanni. This retribution serves to incinerate every self-indulgence as well as my nostalgia for the past, which still exists. It crouches and springs out suddenly, to make me lament the time when I was young and pretty, while now I'm here, immobilized and forced to stew in my own juices. I remember how I used to like to travel, how I could pick out differences among countries and cities. No longer can there be the happy, adventurous abandon that came from traveling in a car with a friend-lover. We would stop to buy cigarettes from one of those dusty, crowded, bazaar-like tobacco stands along the road, and then leave joking, in the early evening light, looking for a restaurant or tavern.

In the sixties I was possessed by the spirit of the times: wanting instant gratification, as if it depended solely on negotiation or on clear and distinct reasoning. As a consequence I was inclined toward truculent and brutal choices.

I had come back from the United States with the rebellion that was simmering, and I had developed a close complicity with three guys my age. Two were very good friends, they were always together; another guy, who lived in the country, in the Langhe, often joined them. I had become the girlfriend of one of the two friends (who had been one of my first loves, the one who was like James Dean), and the group had reconstituted itself as a foursome. Together we sought to put into practice a revolutionary aspiration: always behave on the borderline of provocation, never telling lies, swearing, wandering around at night, reading scandalous novelists and poets. We had an old Fiat 600, in which we went to visit our friend in the Langhe, the setting for our myths. We would go off again with him, screeching through hills and taverns, in search of places where we could taste wines and have contests to guess their vintages. We dreamed of finding a house in a little green valley and living there together, working the land, listening to music, writing, and studying.

The three of us had rented an apartment in the city where we attended the university; one room each, very little furniture: beds, tables, lots of chairs, more versatile than any other furnishings. We pursued disorder in a literal sense: the plates remained unwashed for weeks and gigantic mold formed. We lived for days and days in poverty, eating only potatoes and

eggs—there was always wine. Suddenly a little money appeared and then: French cheeses, sumptuous feasts. Many friends and classmates passed through our loose household, and every once in a while sought refuge there from their families; they slept on mattresses on the floor or in the bath tub. It was open warfare with the building custodian.
Enjoying good food, the highly refined Piedmontese cuisine, truffles, was in happy contrast with a general orientation that rejected social gratifications, careers, human respect. Sometimes we cooked for an entire afternoon, a colossal fritto misto for example, with all the ingredients tradition demanded.

In the midst of this chaos and filth I continued to dress like a lady. I used to go with my girlfriend to a dressmaker who copied French patterns for us, and we had dresses made for ourselves in coordinated colors and styles: mine beige with white patterns and hers black with beige patterns, or else two very similar tailored suits but in different shades. It was a game suggested by our shared provincial background and based on another complicity, between girls. Men looked at us, propositioned us. We laughed: "I prefer my friend," with reciprocal coyness. The disguise continued in our make-up, eyes shaded in white and black, no rouge. The eye make-up took time and skill, with the white pencil and the white inside the eye too. It was very striking and created a waif-like look. My two friends couldn't stand neckties and refused to put them on for important occasions. These things, which elicited stares or reactions of annoyance, were enough to keep us on our toes, feeding our need to transgress. In our relationships with others mockery was the constant tone.

The transgressions of subsequent years would open other doors to self-destruction for younger generations. At the time some smoked dope occasionally, without much conviction. We disparaged it as too remote from our literary tradition, which was Pavesian and Piedmontese.
Our biggest transgression was the free exercise of sexuality. We had read a lot of Henry Miller, we read Wilhelm Reich. We were convinced that orgasm combatted the repression of bourgeois society, in addition to demolishing "character armor." Relationships immediately became sexualized, especially when they were intense. It was the idea of breaking down barriers, of doing everything, on the basis of a commitment: "un-dramatize sexuality, enough of all these deliberations: virginity or not, to fuck or not. When one person wants to he or she says so," and the ideal response was: "Why not?" We had learned this formula from Simone de Beauvoir, or rather, from Sartre, who had reacted to her an-

nouncement that she wanted to spend a year with Nelson Algren in Chicago thus: "Pourquoi pas?" Based on these two little words one could do many apparently senseless things. The idea was to destroy. Abolish the connection between sexuality and love, reject the family, violate fidelity. The student life, afternoons wasted: "So, what shall we do, shall we go to Superga?" "Yeah, let's go," or else "And if we were to make love?" "Let's do it." Often it was a mere exercise, an experiment that had to do with the head, not with pleasure or desire.

I had a role model, a character in one of Lawrence Durrell's novels, Justine. I had been impressed by her wandering through the slums of Alexandria, untouched and unreachable amid that misery, not belonging to anyone despite her furious insistence on using her body freely. Someone guarded her secretly, her husband Nessim, who had her followed both to protect her and to keep track of her without forbidding her anything. In the sequels, what seemed like an erotic obsession turned out to be dictated by political motivations, in a conspiracy shared with her husband. Her body was no longer just the instrument for the annihilation of the moral current within herself, but also a means for obscure collective ends, for intrigue and liberation on behalf of a secret community. I didn't know then that Justine could be the latest incarnation of the gnostic Sophia, the feminine face of God, his/her wisdom and madness, lost in the desire to be like the father and only of the father, capable of alternating asceticism and orgy. Like her, we too felt thrust into a hostile world; we were few in number, characterized by our suffering and our extraneousness to the blind masses. We too felt our alienation from the world and the desire to make that world disappear.

Another ideal figure in the new female empyrean was the Marquise de Merteuil, with her cold-blooded precepts: flit from one love affair to another with a savoir faire that conceals the heartlessness and glorifies the shrewdness—at the time it seemed to me like intelligence—of the plot, flaunting one's skepticism and relativism concerning emotions. Every bond was dangerous: better to replace it with calculation, or declarations of intent.

 But the primary example continued to be Simone de Beauvoir. She and Sartre did the things we would have liked to do: they wrote, they traveled, they lived in hotels rather than in homes. They were stoic and materialist, they were free and extreme, without a future. They had affairs with others, but they told each other everything, sharing the world in their omnivorous coupling. And yet they marked the persistence of distance by using the vous rather than the tu with each other. We too, my boyfriend and I, *attempted to put those models into practice. In doing so we jeopardized our affection, our reciprocal admiration, the possibility for deep understanding.*

Out of all that was born a violent notion of liberty, an extremism that concealed a certain self-hatred. Be done with the image of the woman-mother, warm and affectionate refuge; assert toughness, coldness, detachment, distance. But the "open" relationship with a man became very closed, the site of fusion between ideas and ideals, of reaction to experiences with other people, of unrecognized sufferings, establishing a hierarchy dominated by the couple.

I don't remember the feeling of jealousy from that period. Something inside me suffered, but it didn't find ways to experience the feeling, it expressed itself silently. After a summer spent in different places, we were supposed to meet one evening in Paris—my boyfriend, my girlfriend (without coordinated clothing that evening), and I. A sexual relationship existed between the two of them as well. While I was waiting for them in a little hotel near the Bibliothèque Nationale, I began to run a very high temperature, which kept me in bed until I returned to Italy. With great good will they brought me food they knew I liked, like paella. I couldn't swallow it with that fever. Fever as jealousy, falling in love as inflammation of the imagination.

APRIL

Easter at the home of friends in Tuscany, among the hills and woods. I resume having limpid dreams, no longer murky; I've become dream-dependent, I can't breathe without them. One: I emerge from deep water, much deeper than I imagined, one level after another, and still further to get out; but clear water, not a struggle, more breath than expected. Another: eggs from which chicks are about to hatch on blue satin, like my last nightgown.

This morning I went out in the garden early, among rosemary and lavender bushes: in front the hill of olive trees, the blue stakes of the vines. Impulse of the imagination that encounters images of men, says confusedly: "How happy we would be here with. . . ." Why do you play these tricks on me? Help me instead, little monkey, imagine other things.

Doing yoga, the first time I resumed after vacation, I sensed that I had had X's head in place of mine, that now I was getting back to myself. Rising slowly to my feet, I was aware of trying to raise his big form, tall and broad-shouldered, and not my own, smaller and more delicate. I believed I was he, I wanted to appropriate him for myself. The top of the head is an especially revealing place, in certain moments: encircled by a black nimbus, by dark clouds, fog and overcast—maybe this is why sometimes I walk stooped over with my head sprinkled with ashes. Today however: a papyrus plant grows on my head.

Amidst dreams and remembrances, I reconstruct a parade of the men in my life. A multifaced god, from the great loves to the men barely desired for their appearances, their glances. What links them? A lost, vacuous, tormented gaze, a blank, out-of-it stare? In men, madness, nothingness, the abyss used to attract me.

Abandon a weak father for strong women. But then keep trying to compensate for his absence by the choice of an ideal and idealized father—ideas—and relationships with men who are mysterious and unattainable or else fleeting and playful, or fluid because of alcohol, created in the image and likeness of an unattainable self. Be attracted to a man who is never there, an emptiness that focuses the gaze in an obsessive manner. Mirror of my own not being there, not making a commitment, giving and taking myself away, popping out like soap grasped in wet hands. To be in myself instead, to love myself, would also mean being capable of realistic loves that allow for existing in the real world, in history, building affections on mutual solidarity.

X phones that he's been sick. My new insights dissolve. I wish I could save him from his pain. One breath is enough to make me relapse: on the phone he starts talking without any preliminaries, as if I knew it would be he.

Last night around two o'clock I awoke, enraged by my love affair. I lay in bed fantasizing for two hours before my anger subsided.
Toward G. as well: "Last time I was momentarily irritated because you were calculating my bill while I was impatient to talk to you." "You've done the right thing to bring it up," it's impossible to upset him. I emphasize that this is the first time I've been angry with him. It is a period in which this state of mind finally appears. G. mentions my desire to keep our relationship insulated from money. I know that paying is an essential part of the relationship. What's strange is that the artificiality, a mercenary relationship, constructed in a laboratory, works. "It's ridiculous to agree to become fond of someone you pay," a friend told me. "But also for it to be reciprocal," I add.

Yesterday afternoon, at four o'clock, already prepared to go to G.'s office, I throw up. Violent heaves, vomit that fails to expel the gluey brown rice from lunch. I had tried to resume the Steiner diet, which I alternate with my Piedmontese diet, because the night before with X I had eaten and drunk too much. Chills, nausea, hours of vomiting. In my convulsions—sitting on the floor, I was afraid I wouldn't make it, palpitations—I experienced the need to expel both this food and this man from inside me. Everything I thought I had digested came back up. Throw up the desire for devotion without limits, absolute availability, renunciation of every freedom.

I only managed to phone G. toward evening. The debate, the session skipped. Face covered with red dots, will they ever go away? According to the doctor it was a hepatic colic. Today is a day for convalescing. Fantasy of being so sick that both X and Dr. G. have to visit me in the hospital. Scene of Violetta dying while the carnival whirls madly in the streets of Paris, and she is alone. Alfredo and his father still haven't arrived, only the doctor is in attendance: "*Ah, un vero amico,*" a true friend, who can't save her from death.

G. follows the sequence on love and vomit with interest. And also a dream in which I had to eat cat shit and spat it out. He questions me about this diet, which had never come up before. I explain to him that during the two years preceding analysis I had strictly followed a personalized Steiner diet, based on squash, onions, brown rice, couscous, and some—not many—greens. Then slowly I went back to foods that everyone eats: with X also back to wine, coffee, salami, and chocolate. Now I alternate the two systems.

I express the conviction that I expelled X and his food together. According to G., however, I expelled the brown rice, which seems to him a bit like Esperanto, artificial and indigestible, more brain than body. But he also says that the problem is more complicated, like going back and forth between two languages until you can no longer speak either one.

Zaira, however, maintains that squash obstructs the liver, to the point that the liver can no longer eliminate it.

X is handsome, affectionate, and happy, he takes me by the arm and escorts me to lunch, ordering the lightest dishes for me. Seeing myself in the mirror of the restaurant I blush at how ugly I look. He realizes it, understands: "You've been sick," he says, "ugliness is something else." But I don't fall for it for an instant.

"I feel some bitterness toward that man," I say to G.
"That's down-to-earth" (i.e., a good sign, in contrast with my propensity for the heavenly).
"Yes, but it means that I haven't fully understood."
" . . . ."
"His behavior has been . . . insensitive."
He agrees.
I want to dismantle my bitterness, untangle it, not allow it to poison me.

I bought myself two silk slips, used, beautiful. I awake thinking: *"fille de soie, fille de soi,"* another pun on the "u." Daughter of myself, mother of myself.

Desire to adorn myself, to take care of myself. Pleasure in my legs with pretty stockings and shoes, pleasure in necklaces, toilet water, and col-ored scarves.

Poor ego, it has practically had to spin wool like Hercules. In my search for femininity, I have literally set it to doing housework. I have broken its pride making it swallow the subordinate position of lover. I have turned down conferences, meetings, I haven't even given it the satisfaction of work.
I had understood the return to femininity as objective: the realm of food, clothes, jewelry, adornment. A comic-strip pink period: transit across tra-ditional femininity. But it was worthwhile to pass through that place. And also: to pass through dishonor.

A woman friend gives me a bunch of pale pink peonies, large and with buds at various stages, harder, softer. Their magnificence, their scent, the heaviness and lightness together of the corollas.

JUNE

I continue not to know what to eat, not to be able to choose between the two nutritional systems. Recollections of old foods: hard biscuits, polenta. Things that once we always ate, now abandoned: a soup of rice and milk, chestnut soup, soup made of semolina, coffee with milk for supper.

I dreamed about a man in Tunisia with the name of my analyst.
"How curious," he says. "Did you know I was in Tunisia?"

I certainly did not know. But it is one of the many "coincidences" that
pop up in analysis during this period. G. again: "Don't get smug about the
coincidences."
Stroll with X along the banks of the Po. By mutual agreement, we see
each other for limited periods of time, outdoors.

I dream that I am going to buy myself a bodysuit in a store for religious
articles.
"Doesn't that seem a bit odd to you," G. grins.
I try to defend the dream and its sexuality as a pantomime of the rela-
tionship with the absolute. The absolute is precisely what G. mistrusts.
A series of associations. An old dream reappears, connected to this one.
G., as if in an aside on stage: "Does looking for a body in religion lead to
eating cat shit?"

JULY

Separation from G. earlier than usual, as we both have to go away. Fare-
well different from last year's. Once again he shares a sadness on my part,
which becomes recognizable and acceptable if it's his too. It's his being
capable of sadness without yielding to it that makes him a good guide.
Our memories and our positions are asymmetrical, but there are shared
paths and places.
I had dreamed about dried fish and potatoes in large quantities. Things to
take along on a sea voyage, modest provisions for someone who is going
to be away a long time.

Oxford. During the meeting, looking at the gray sky, in contrast, the colors that have dominated my analysis in recent months—dreams, discussion, clothes—jump out: violet, lilac, fuchsia, bordeaux. For me they are
symbols of the union between red and blue, between passion and reason,
between near and far.

Tonight at dinner, fish and potatoes—but in England that's not hard. I wit-
ness the slow separation between the voice of G. and that of the "u."
A bed of peonies at St. John's College: red-violet, rose-colored and white.

Service in the cathedral at Oxford, with a chorus of boys and young men,
very solemn. The gospel, of Luke, included the parables of the man who
finds the lost lamb and the woman who finds the piece of silver. Divert

this all for oneself, recover the objectified in religion and turn it back into subjectivity. That's how I perceive myself: in a phase of rediscovery. But I can't reappear too soon: fishes and potatoes are under the surface.

Walk with Fay in Waterloo Park, both of us with hay fever. We buy ourselves two boxes made from the same piece of wood. She is the only person with whom I discuss my analysis, and vice versa; we started our analyses at the same time and, although very different, they are proceeding with some parallels. We catch up with each other every six or eight months, with a few postcards in between. There are older parallels as well: a shared love for the green world of Oz, in particular for the window that shifted landscape continually and for the possibility of changing heads. I also tell her the story of Belinda and the white roses, evidence for me of the impossible love with the father.
Talking with Fay, other parts of my life emerge, which I generally leave in the shadows. They are easier to talk about in English, they lose some of their shamefulness; here I can deal with myself as if seeing myself from afar.

In the mid-sixties the peer group, the gang, split up. A passion between me and the third companion, who had been the close friend of my boyfriend, had intervened. Inevitable, because it was the only forbidden thing. Between us there was possible an abandon, physical as well, such as I had never known and of which I was perhaps not capable, except for short periods. That affair lasted a few months, interrupted by my grandmother's death and by my abortion. I didn't experience pain at the death of the grandmother who had raised me, I didn't cry, I didn't feel grief. Perhaps some rancor still survived because of the fact that so many years before she had hidden my mother's death from me, letting me believe for months that she was recuperating in a hospital in another city. The decision to have an abortion was automatic: I had never planned to have children, it was totally outside my horizon. It took place in the clandestine circumstances of the time: problems coming up with the money, a kitchen table, pain that seared my insides. My boyfriend who waited for me outside with a tormented face; the solitude of my subsequent thoughts.
The couple reconstituted itself on the basis of these events, ever closer and richer. I would have given the world for that understanding, it would have been surprising if I couldn't sacrifice love for it. Thus we made the mistake of repressing the things that endangered our union rather than accepting the contradictions, of wanting to restore the fusion rather than acknowledging the cracks. I was weakened by three losses, unaware of

having endured any loss and of suffering from it. My language began to
reflect cynicism and bitterness; I used harsh terms, dry or biting expressions, I was hypercritical, derisive, cutting.

A contemporary cultural climate reinforced this attitude in me. I attended
the faculty of philosophy, finding compatible with my state of mind the
teaching of a professor-maestro who mocked every metaphysics, broke
with transcendence, insisted on the preciseness of language, even of pro-
nunciation. Relativism of all cultures, attention to the advanced points of
the social sciences, horror at every redundancy, which was prevalent in
other teachers. Existentialism in its original negativism was softened, but
kept as a starting point: the possibility of putting oneself at ground zero
of existence. The fascination of his teaching also lay in the contradiction
between the elegance and vitality of his person—in his speech, in his
gestures, in his thinking—and the negativity of some of his messages.
They were messages of emancipation, which invited one to free oneself
from every dogma, and they revealed an intolerance for everything that
couldn't be stated in precise terms; they advocated going all out in taking
words literally, but also making short shrift of any reflection toward the
unspoken. Perhaps in his students the balance tilted and we tended to
wield what we considered the razor of reason too quickly.

Under the pressure of the times, we turned to politics, a politics I could
accept without ceasing to make fun of politics and its values. In 1963 the
architecture faculty had been occupied. A huge banner flew over the Valentino castle; inside sleeping bags, guitars, long discussions about city
planning (which was not yet taught) and the connection between architecture and politics.

Four friends and I discovered the writings of the Situationist International.
We identified with the mocking attitude, the nullifying gesture of the
"happening" that disrupts solemn cultural ceremonies, the obstinacy of
those who take their adversaries literally in order to show up the emptiness of those adversaries. The ostentatious exercise of intelligence
seduced us, while we made fun of all the most prominent intellectuals.
The certainty of internationalism, already a reality, that didn't create hierarchies among first, second, and third world, excited us. The uprisings in
the black ghettos of the United States, where there was looting, showed
that capitalism was being taken at its word, advertising was being un-
masked along with the product, utilized and undramatized at the same
time. We also liked the emphasis on having the best (and contemporaneously the denigration of the best: the journal of the Situationist International had glossy paper, photos, shiny covers); the ideal of the "situationist compromise," which in the choice between two goods opted

for both; the détournement *that inserted the words of Marx in the most widely read comics. We practiced "drifting"—letting ourselves flow with the urban currents and then analyzing the implications of the results—as a critique of urban life, which was part of the critique of alienated every-day life.*

In 1966 we went to Strasbourg, where some students and some situation-ists had taken over the student government and used it to demystify that structure. They spent the funds on the publication of a pamphlet, "On Misery in the Student Environment," which we translated into Italian with a preface on revolution as party and game, adding the usual situationist formula which renounced any copyright.

We had formed a little philo-situationist group (we never joined the orga-nization, thus avoiding being expelled, as inevitably happened), which at the beginning of '67 wrote a document on daily revolution and presented it at a conference on "The Student Movement, Class Culture, Political Struggle." The group—composed of the usual five of us—had a post of-fice box and called itself "Group One," I don't remember why. Certainly not in the hope that others would follow, because one of the tenets was the proud certainty that there were only a few of us. A recurrent adjective in that document was "laughable," applied primarily to the "progressives of the left" who proposed reforms of the university and the system; equally laughable were free time, vacations, all the illusions created by the "spectacle" industry. We used provocative terms such as "the meno-pause of the intelligence" and "the Resistance Mafia," to refer to leftist in-tellectuals. When we presented the document at the meeting, in Verona —I made the presentation, dressed completely in black as I had taken to doing in that period—we created a bit of a scandal. One of our former high school teachers, anti-Fascist and militant in the PSIUP (Socialist Party of Proletarian Unity), chided us, pointing out the similarities be-tween our verbal extremism and that of early Fascism.

Following the conference we had a meeting in Milan with the group from the Negative University of Trent, much larger than our group. Debate to the bitter end: some of them were taking methedrine to stay awake and waste less of their lives sleeping. At the end of an exhausting day, Renato Curcio, who later became a leader of the Red Brigades and spent many years in jail, suddenly broke in and announced that he had figured out the fundamental difference dividing the two groups: "You're not Leninists?!" he accused in an almost interrogatory tone, considering the seriousness of the matter. We confirmed that not only were we not Leninists, we weren't even Marxists in the sense that they were. We came together around a common vision of the world, a desire for the subversion and critique of

respectability and for a break with it. Our companions in Trent were in-transigent: given that divergence it was useless to go on arguing.
Our little group—down from five to four because one didn't agree with our praxis—met with the young people from a working-class neighbor-hood, who had organized an exhibit on Vietnam and a fundraising drive for the National Liberation Front. We would meet them in the square after supper and argue about imperialism, criticize the idea of the party, dis-cuss politics. They demonstrated a stubborn desire to persevere in the situation in which they found themselves—that square, those people, that daily routine—but they insisted on putting their situation into the context of worldwide problems. By now this was the spirit of the times. The young people of the square were from working-class backgrounds; be-tween them and us a mutual attraction developed such as often springs up between people of different classes, especially between workers and intellectuals. Compared to us they had been politicized much longer, be-ginning with the FGCI (Italian Communist Youth Federation), but they were shaking off that background. We were just approaching politics at the time, and thus we met half-way. We were all equally polemical with respect to the PCI (Italian Communist Party), which nonetheless offered us rooms in its headquarters for continuing our discussions when it was raining.

AUGUST

I take shelter in the house in Tuscany where I can always return, among the trees, friends, silence. X is on vacation with his family and there's no phone here.
Crossing the patio in the sun—jasmine and hibiscus flowers—catching sight of an ant on the little wall of the terrace tinged with pink and grey mildew: gratitude, today there is time, there is relief from the alternating joy and pain of the past months.

Every morning I labor to assemble the montage of interviews for the En-glish book on the generation of '68. Mechanically, adhering to the cri-teria given.

Dream black-out; is the "u" on vacation too?

Zaira and I compare the panic that certain images of femininity provoke in us. For me: images that embody laziness, slothfulness, coquettishness, cunning, frivolity, exclusion from public life. For her: the great obscure mother, unmoving and disapproving.

Something is coming to an end after having been strongly reactualized in a way that didn't seem bearable to me: nostalgia for my peer group. I'm really finished with love among equals: the adolescents, the friends, the Dioscuri, the players, the students, the couple that laughs at the world, existing in a relationship of alliance and competition. Now love is experience of the other, more other than that I couldn't bear.

Frugality, repetition, reconciliation. The smell of medicinal herbs gathered in the garden, sage laurel thyme, stabilize, restore, just as the taste of tea at times.

Now solitude might begin to make sense. Not the sense of the ultimate goal, but one in progress, so to speak: it's a matter of reaching a clearing, an open space, where affections are sparse and vigorous, an expanse sufficient for measuring my life.
The regret at not being young any longer, at seeing the signs of aging in my face and body, also becomes less sharp. Life begins to lay itself out on a plane of equidistance, it's no longer completely spasmodic, it crumbles from past to present independently of me. However, I always have an absence to mourn, this time my analysis. I have begun to fear losing my place with G.

I return home. Intense solitude, it's like death, no one can experience it in my place.
A dream appears, but so simple that I wonder if I have really dreamed it or if it weren't rather a moment of torpor: a fly and a mosquito that intertwine their flights along a diagonal that ascends like my convolvulus on the balcony. Knotted, curved, circular trajectories, certainly not linear paths. Parasitic, useless, and harmful animals. But also jesting, light, distracted.
Thus the "u" makes its presence known again, with the subtlest whine of the vilest insects, which the world is full of and which we squash without giving it a thought. "U" as un-knowable and un-graspable and un-predictable. A message even more tenuous than that of being like the birds of the air: let yourself go like a gnat, without ceremony, but insistent, ineradicable. I miss G.'s laugh.
Distinct sensation that in dying I would have to leave everything: books, clothes, friends, if death came up now from the warm, noisy, summer street. I would be sorry because of some paths I have yet to travel, like the

one with G., because of a book I would like to write, because of a friend's baby I would like to see grow up.

An evening with X, of the kind he likes, without future, without prospects, suspended in the void. My obsession with the phone has resumed.

Dream about freeing handicapped children from a hospital in a deep valley. They run up the slope of snow, shrieking with joy, an unfettered joy. There is a small child, who could also be one of the handicapped, but in the dream's vision he is pretty and healthy, dressed in a greenish blue tee-shirt. I hesitate to invite him, I'm afraid he'll be a burden on the journey; then I call to him affectionately, in English, "Come on, kid." He exhibits the greatest joy, genuine, pure—I've never seen such a joy—and we set off: he's good, pretty, he radiates an unforgettable contentment. But we still have to deal with the bad guys, a rival gang.

SEPTEMBER

G. has returned. I had some uncertainties at our first meeting: between July and August, despite the period of the black-out, there were almost one hundred dreams, according to my quick calculation. After having talked a bit at random, I hit on the image of the joyful child as the constant. "Maybe it's because of the joy," G. reflects.
Is it for joy that one goes through analysis? besides for sharing sadness?

I dream about a change in the room where we meet, in the chaises longues, with G. behind me. A circle around the other person, which perhaps is reaching its completion?

A sense of prosperity emerges in the mere eating of basic food while listening to music, a perception once again, after many years, of the splendor of the most unexpected things, the frames of my eyeglasses marbled with red, the sparkle of the faucets in the bathroom, the dish of olives on the table.

OCTOBER

I start working a lot again. But a breach between the ego and the identity

has developed. I am no longer anything specific, I am a mix of full and empty, a slippery and uneven footbridge on the river. I am not my work, nor a love affair, nor a political project. In this inner theater there is not one who directs, but an entire unhinged company of performers, with their gags and crass quips.
The short circuit between the internal image and X has cracked as well.

Yesterday with G. a meeting disrupted: by his need to prepare the bill, by flies, by two phone calls, by the doorbell. To some extent, I'm irked, to some extent I feel it's all part of the process.

X comes for dinner, I tell him I don't love him anymore, he doesn't believe it. Tough evening, of opposition, almost physical. But it's true. Not like before.

In the market I find white roses at a good price. The *puella* recovers her position, fed up with the excesses of Griselda. But I want a woman's destiny, not a girl's.

Recurring dream of the mailboxes in my grandmother's old house, under the entryway. In the dream it wasn't clear if the mailbox was mine or not, if the notice inside was really for me.

NOVEMBER AND DECEMBER

The more detached and critical I am, the nicer X is. He gets momentarily irritated only when I tell him that I don't detect in him any effect of his analysis, that it seems to me he does it only when he has nothing better to do, with the excuse of all his trips and an accommodating analyst. But he drops the subject.

Confusion, stagnation, suspension. Lots of work.

G. is pleased, he practically applauds when I tell him I have become an associate professor. In this way my financial situation is also becoming healthy.

I have no desire for another Christmas alone, I accept an invitation to Cambridge from old friends from Africa. A regular family, parents and two children, who host various singles for Christmas, like Eric and me, after so many years.

To reject everything, gain some distance from everything, this was the feeling that had impelled me to Africa and before that into situationism, into opposition in other words, in the illusion of finding myself outside and opposed. A strong sense of boredom with everything, especially with myself; desire to extinguish myself, to deny, to nullify.

I had left thinking I wouldn't return. I had sold everything I owned, from my science fiction collection to my furniture and the property left by my grandmother. It didn't seem as if I was leaving much: after graduation I had lived on fellowships, translations, research for the C.N.R.
We had gone for adventure, for third world conviction, and because my companion wanted to substitute civil service for his military service. We didn't know exactly what we were going to do. We were pursuing the revolution, popular struggles, the memory of the Resistance. Before leaving I went to talk to my old partisan friends: they told me how to make a fuse, how to blow up a car on a macadam road. Fortunately—considering my total ineptitude—we never got involved in such things.
At first we lived in Kenya, where we become friends with some members of the opposition party; but it was reduced to powerlessness, in an oppressive and desultorily illiberal cultural and political climate. Then I moved by myself to Dar es Salaam, where I finally understood how I could be useful. I put my sociohistorical knowledge and my ability to write in several languages at the disposition of Frelimo—the Mozambique Liberation Front—and they used it for informational and propaganda purposes both inside and outside the country. It was wonderful and exciting work, with extraordinary people, enlivened by their own creativity and that of others; mutual recognition made the tremendous difficulties tolerable. My Mozambican companions were grateful to me for having gathered, literally off the ground, the poems written by militants of every rank, in Portuguese mixed with African languages. The poems were strewn everywhere in the old headquarters on the Morogoro Road in Dar; I gathered them the way I collected political documents, I reflected on them and I wrote about them, trying to fit them into a history of the liberation of Mozambique and its people. Not having a home any longer, I saw my ideal of being a vagabond realized; I was a guest by turns of various friends and acquaintances; the houses were large, on the university campus it was always possible to find places to stay.
After that I moved to Zambia to put together a collection of similar materials on Zimbabwe and South Africa, without the close collaboration I had enjoyed with Frelimo. I remember my wanderings through the African

districts of Lusaka, with no street names, looking for little-known groups and movements, interviewing old South African exiles with Trotskyite roots. I remember debates with the young people from the two opposing parties, Zapu and Zanu. I felt close to the second, although I supported Zapu, in accord with the line that favored Frelimo, the ANC in South Africa, Zapu in Zimbabwe, the MPLA in Angola over the opposing parties. But the young people from Zanu spoke a language I recognized: verbal violence, mistrust of Europe, from its governments to its Communist parties, leftist critique of the American Black Power movement. I argued interminably about the Zanu/Zapu opposition with my hosts, who had spent a long time in Zimbabwe doing anthropological field research. It was one case in which the choice between two antagonistic movements turned out to be more difficult, less convincing.

In Lusaka I had met Eric, just escaped from the dreadful South African prison in which he had been held in solitary confinement. I was living at the time with a friend who taught English literature at the university. We were rather far from the city, in a beautiful stone house managed by a Zambian major-domo by the name of Simons. Simons observed with a critical eye my lack of Englishness, particularly evident in my breakfast habits. While I was a guest there, they organized a party, for which they prepared kegs of African beer and roasted goats on the grass in front of the house. Some of the black guests laughed because in dishing out the meat the men got some parts that traditionally would have gone to women and vice versa. While I was trying to filter through my teeth the beer made with coarse flour, which I drank for Africanism, Eric appeared. He offered me some wine he had brought. It couldn't have been either Portuguese or South African because we were boycotting products from both those countries. It was French wine, which Eric uncorked carefully and tasted before offering it to me. He drank it with intense pleasure, closing his eyes, quoting Homer on the wine-colored Mediterranean.

Those moments of relaxation interrupted an atmosphere of violence and tension, in which suspicions, intrigues, and squabbles alternated. We saw the CIA everywhere and often it really was there; some individuals were known agents and this was accepted as standard procedure. The political attacks were a pressing reality. I had met the president of Frelimo, Edward Mondlane. One night at his house there had been lengthy discussions of his political education and literacy projects for the liberated areas. The next morning one of the friends present at the meeting the evening before came to see me: the president had been blown up by a letter bomb.

After that assassination there was an acceleration in the process of disintegration within the community of white radicals that revolved around

*the university, around the liberation movements that had their head-
quarters in Dar, around the progressive milieus of the Tanzanian government. The latter no longer renewed our visas, discouraged us from staying on.*

*I moved to Cairo, continuing with my collection of political documents
and informational materials. At the time there were interesting people in
Cairo, some from Frelimo and some Angolans whom I wanted to meet
because they did not belong to recognized movements and were supported by the Peoples' Republic of China. But in Cairo too I had the growing sense that the role of white sympathizers was increasingly tenuous,
demonstrating the limits of our voluntarism that abandoned the cities of
the world for the countrysides of the oppressed.*

*Those had been years of great hopes, of strong friendships, of the convic-
tion that we were contributing to the creation of new cultures and new
individuals, especially in Dar, which at that time had many diplomatic
missions, including those from Cuba, from China, from Vietnam. Their
presence raised the tone of the political environment in the city, it made
us feel as if we were in direct contact with those countries undergoing
transformations, it heightened the feeling of a great common undertaking
in which it was necessary to take sides, to struggle, to give without reser-
vation. All this on the backdrop of the eastern coast of Africa, with its
Arab and African traditions. I remember the brightly colored market in
Dar, swimming in the sea in the evenings with the huge full moon, and
the old colonial hotels where there was a profusion of languages spoken:
still a smattering of German, a bit of French, that liquid, sibilant Portuguese, Swahili in all its forms, from the poor and base to the most elaborate, with lengthy rhymed terms for translating foreign words, and above
it all, British and American English. Maybe we even hoped that out of that
Tower of Babel a new language would emerge, one that everyone would
know how to speak and understand. In addition to the mixture of tongues,
the mixture of different bodies was remarkable, black brown blond hair
and skin, the ample outfits made of vivid African materials for the humid
heat that was debilitating but also allowed one to sleep less, to live every
moment of life with fervor. The intellectual enthusiasm was intense, the
debates heated, the political oppositions vehement.*

*In a country where you are a stranger either because you come from far
away or because, although born there, you have become estranged from
your country as a result of colonialism, you could delude yourself about
creating new fatherlands, new civilizations beyond Maoist and populist
ideologies. Many people from that time have remained in my life. My
friend Zaira, the anthropologists and the literature teacher from Lusaka
now in Peking, Eric, others too, scattered in various places around the*

world, often in motion. We see each other after years and right away it's like yesterday, even if all our hopes and illusions of establishing a different world in Africa, a world free from the restrictions of the blocs, capable of launching an African culture aware of its cultural precedents, have collapsed.

While I was taking part in all this in the third world, 1968 was happening in the first world.

Why talk about something I didn't share, in what's supposed to be an autobiography, albeit a collective autobiography? Why this interpretation from an absence that does not permit the use of the plural subject and requires a tone that is more objective even if fraught with subjectivity? Because '68 is the validation of something that we, who are a few years older, experienced and vaguely prefigured in the preceding period; it's the transition from the few to the many, if not yet to a majority, from the individual to the collective, from private to public. And also because there is a vein of '68 acknowledged as a worldwide phenomenon that changed and will change the course of our lives, within a process that is not completed and is thus difficult to grasp. Reconstructing it is a way of continuing it and of detecting the next steps.

One 1968

Democracy, Power, Knowledge

On November 27, 1967, the students in the humanities faculties at the University of Turin occupied their building, the Palazzo Campana, and communicated to the professors of letters, philosophy, political science, teachers' training, and law their decision to

> throw completely open for debate the didactic structure and the scientific and cultural content of university teaching and the criteria on which examinations are based.

The genesis of this agitation was the decision of the University Administrative Council to acquire the "La Mandria" area and house the science faculties there. Above all, the students attacked the method adopted by the academic authorities as "privatistic, authoritarian, unscientific," because it didn't take into account the demands made by the student movement regarding the relationships between university and environment, between the faculties of humanities and those of the sciences, between academic reform and university construction.

But the protest went far beyond the spark that had ignited it. Its main content quickly became the demand for a new and different learning, the critique of authoritarianism, the establishment of spaces for communal discussion and communal life. The takeover of Palazzo Campana was the culmination of a long series of struggles and the beginning of a radically new phase. Since the end of the fifties Italian universities had experienced protests over the question of reform, which criticized government projects and often put forth alter-

62

native proposals. In the sixties the demands were interspersed with the organization of courses on anti-imperialist topics, against authoritarian regimes and in support of liberation struggles in Asia, Africa and Latin America.

While many of the struggles prior to '68 had involved takeovers, the peculiar characteristics and possibilities of the technique had not been emphasized. With the occupation of Palazzo Campana, elements present in the earlier takeovers were further developed and clarified to make it an instrument of work, of reflection, of consciousness-raising. In reality, at that historical moment, because of the collective life it encouraged, the takeover contained within itself a push toward democracy, toward equality, toward radical participation.

Herein lie some of the reasons for the interest that '68 holds for the present, especially an experience like Turin's, where the link between free speech and subjectivity had particular significance. This link was not the only theme in the complex phenomenon that was Turin 1968, nor was it foreign to student movements in other cities. In other countries it actually appeared earlier or more forcefully and more extensively, as in the cases of the University of California at Berkeley and May 1968 in France. But in Turin the relationship between personal and political manifested itself with all its idiosyncracies and clarities, which are directly tied to the comprehensive path we are exploring. Precisely in order to stick to that path, I will single out from the context of the city one specific 1968, that of the humanities faculties, where the themes that interest us assumed greatest importance.

The occupation of Palazzo Campana called into question the authoritarian structure hidden "behind the mask of neutrality of science and of culture." It posited the question of democracy both politically, on the level of the management of the university, and intellectually. The first led to reclaiming decision-making power for elements of the university other than the narrow circle of tenured professors, the "barons." Therefore, it involved and replayed, rather more dramatically and radically than in the union-oriented movements of the preceding years, the protests of those teachers referred to as "subordinates," such as the nontenured professors and especially the assistants. The participation of the latter in the Turin agitation was not terribly widespread, but it made an important contribution and doubtless was extremely significant in the eyes of the students and of public opinion.

The demands for democracy were so radical that the academic authorities could not satisfy them: the Turin movement called for direct democracy, which did not permit the delegation of representation. The assemblies had to be the decision-making body, the only counterpart proposed in negotiations with the Academic Senate. Many of the dialogues between the senate and the protesting students ran aground on the senate's refusal to accept the assembly as interlocutor, its insistence on the requirement of recognized representatives, unacceptable to the students.

The link democracy/authority couldn't fail to have repercussions within the movement itself. The aspiration to direct democracy meant that coordinating committees or protest committees named by the assemblies were always considered provisional; and it meant enlarging the membership of these committees, opening up their meetings, and debating everything all over again in the assemblies and commissions. This in turn gave rise to contradictory signals. Too little attention was paid to the different capabilities of individuals for expressing themselves in an assembly or on a commission. Although it was soon clear that the general assembly was an "alienating place," there were always "unresolved problems of democratic management" (Luigi Bobbio). The absence of any institutional acknowledgment of forms of authority highlighted the role of charismatic figures. The idea of democracy as participation with equal rights of speech for individuals was also called into question by a certain movement elitism, by the conviction of being different, of opposing the consensus, the broad majorities, the established order, and social hypocrisy.

All this emerged clearly apropos of the referendum held in November. As a consequence of tumultuous mass meetings and brawls incited by groups of right-wing youths, all the students in Palazzo Campana had agreed to the vote. "The method of the referendum," wrote Peppino Ortoleva several months later, "was accepted only because of demagoguery: it, like all methods of indirect 'democracy,' was denounced on theoretical lines as unrepresentative."

The voting was on two motions. The first, from the right, although negatively assessing the takeover, sustained the necessity—prior to ending the occupation—of making use of the contractual strength resulting from it to negotiate immediately with the Academic Senate regarding a minimum program. The second motion, signed by Viale, Donat Cattin, and Vaudagna, who represented respectively the left, the Catholics, and the liberals, reaffirmed the commitment to the occupation of Palazzo Campana and singled out the student assemblies as the true expression of grass-roots democracy and the fundamental organizational instrument of the student movement. It accepted the referendum in order to demonstrate that even among the students

who did not participate directly in the occupation there was no substantial opposition to that form of struggle. The first motion received
428 votes, the second 815, with 7 blank ballots.

Within the majority camp, however, there were many perplexities
regarding the referendum, and not only perplexities of a theoretical
nature like that mentioned by Ortoleva. Some accounts affirm that
there was a fear of losing as a result of respect for the old notion of
democracy, which rewarded numbers over direct participation. Mistrust of the student masses also lay at the root of these fears; as one
of the students who supported the second motion, Maria Teresa Fenoglio, remembers, tempering '68's values with today's reflection:

> I was absolutely convinced that we were a domineering minority,
> instead I discovered that this was not the case. We all discovered it
> wasn't the case. We had a guilty conscience, because we said we were
> democratic, but we were very authoritarian, even in the mass meet-
> ings. We felt the greatest contempt for those who made up the famous
> silent majority, the sheep—think about the May poster with the sheep
> returning to normality—so much so that we assumed they would vote
> against it.
> Because of that I voted twice in the referendum. I put on two different
> outfits. In my history there has been the presence of another part of
> myself, that I profoundly despised, the girl from a good family, who
> had the suitor and who had the fur coat given to her by her mother and
> the strand of pearls. Because of that I probably identified with the
> silent majority at the university. I went and dressed up like them,
> exactly like them: "Look, I've put on my fur. Look, I've put on my last
> year's glasses." I went to vote first as a sixty-eighter, and then as silent
> majoritarian.

Everyone fought over the silent majority; the rector, *La Stampa,*
and the right-wing antioccupation groups all courted it. The protesting students had a double-edged relationship with the silent majority: of contempt and fear, because they projected onto them a continuity without renewal; of respect and protection, because they were
a "people," oppressed and manipulated by the professors. This mythical majority didn't turn out to vote however. The number of voters,
1,225, is far from the number of students enrolled (around 20,000)
and does not even represent twice the number of those who usually
joined the protests ("there were never more than 700 people at the
general assemblies," Luigi Bobbio).

The double soul symbolically attributed to '68 and experienced by one protagonist via her change of clothes sends us back to the dichotomy present in the roots claimed by this generation. The dichotomy, which originally was ambivalence toward received values (from its fathers, from the Resistance), turned into the necessity of leaping beyond every continuity with the past. But the duality was not lost; rather, it transformed itself into a new contradiction, between rejection of its roots and subterranean lengthening of those roots. Antihistoricism, tendency toward nihilism, intolerance of any authority carried with them, in the very virulence of the polemic, a continuity with respect to the past.

The consequence in any event is duplicity, contradiction, ambivalence, and often polyvalence. Hence a frequent phenomenon of '68: a striking of apparently miraculous balances between opposites, but these balances are ephemeral because they already contain the seeds of their own opposites. This is the case with the relationship between libertarianism and authoritarianism within the movement, between the new possibility of speaking out available to everyone and the different weight carried by the words of some. Thus could democracy end up as pseudo-democracy, a pretense of parity without acknowledgment of the disparities, and it did so in subsequent decades.

The second fundamental link, that between learning and democracy, did not escape the confusions of the first, between democracy and political power. The theme of knowledge was addressed in the experience of the counter-courses. Here, one studied subjects not previously taught in the university, and, most important, one studied in a different way, establishing different relationships with teachers and books. The counter-courses, which simultaneously represented opportunities for alternative discussions and an elementary organizational structure, no longer imitated the traditional division of learning reflected by faculty and institute designations; they were organized around topics such as "Vietnam," "School and Society," "Youth and Protest," "Pedagogy of Dissent," "Psychoanalysis and Social Repression." They disputed not only the form of transmission of knowledge but its political and social function in existing society, the relationships between learning and power.

In the early documents of the takeover there are references to the psychological bases that make the exercise of democracy in the field of knowledge necessary and possible:

One doesn't argue before the authority (and the teacher is an authority); students are intimidated, afraid, bashful in front of the professor, or they simply don't feel they're up to the teacher's level. In order to learn how to argue it's necessary to be among equals, it's necessary to eliminate discrepancies in power between teacher and learner completely.

The students occupying Palazzo Campana . . . are succeeding for the first time in expressing themselves freely in the presence of the assistants who have joined in the occupation, because they feel themselves among equals, united in the same struggle for the conquest of their own didactic and cultural autonomy. ("The Commissions on Study as an Instrument of Protesting Academic Power," December 5, 1967)

Allara and Grosso manage to fill the lecture halls for their classes with the *fear* of roll calls and attendance sheets: they base their domination over the students on the *terror* of their exams.
But what sense is there in a university based on terror, where we don't learn anything except to obey?
It's easy to seize freedom for ourselves: *just disobey.* (Leaflet "To the first-year law students," from "The occupying students," undated)

The critique of the oral exam as a form of evaluation reveals attention to the everyday aspects of the learning relationship: flyers and papers dissect in great detail the relationship between teacher and student, the idiosyncrasies of individual professors; they provide advice on how to sit, what expression to adopt, how to speak, how to make it appear that one knows something in the course of the exam. When the exams resumed, there was also a commitment to monitor them, checking for the "greatest regularity" in the composition of exam committees (traditionally incomplete) and in the procedures.

The topic of intellectual subordination carried out in an unfair fashion (and of the ways of overcoming it) constituted a major attraction for many rank-and-file students, playing on the lack of respect and democracy practiced by many teachers.

Anna Trautteur (born 1945, Turin):
This friend of mine and I participated right from the beginning, because we felt we were a party to this cause, we felt involved, and we were in agreement with the things that were the basic motivations. Having always attended classes, we had realized how many things didn't add up, even if we liked to study and prepare for our exams. We were very lively, so to some extent we did it making fun of ourselves and others, but with respect to certain programs there really was a lot to get mad about. Experiences like an exam with Getto, where we had the handicap of coming from the philosophy faculty, and thus being

viewed unfavorably. I'll always remember Professor Getto saying, "It's a continued waste of time questioning you, you're from philosophy, you don't understand anything." Or else exams like Lana's, in Latin literature. I had taken a course that I had really liked, a survey of literature of the Neronian age. At the exam we had to translate a passage he gave us, and it was Lucan's *Pharsalia.* While I was translating I made a mistake, which I realized immediately. I stopped and said, "Oh, excuse me." I went back and started over, and he threw me out. Absurdities, with yelling like, "Who passed you in your Maturity exam?" When I showed up at the September session, I absolutely had not prepared again, I heard them say to me: "Ah, congratulations, you're a person who really knows her Latin."

Some famous passages of an article by Guido Viale, exposing "the consensual root of authoritarianism" and the possibility of severing it with struggle, also argued against the "psychological conditioning and manipulation of students." His assertions that "books are at least as authoritarian as teachers" created a scandal, as did his provocative way of attacking "bookish culture," describing the activity of some study groups:

The commission "Psychoanalysis and Repression" has decided it is not required to read the book by Adorno and Horkheimer, *The Dialectic of the Enlightenment,* solely because it was written, printed, translated and sold in numerous copies, and devoted itself to more interesting activities. . . . The readings constituted only one component with respect to the discussion work among the members of the commission and between them and the "expert" invited periodically.

Experts came to be denied the honor of authority; they were to be utilized for the concepts they could supply, but without any "intimidation and subordination." Honor and veneration were withdrawn from the book as well:

In recent years, from the economic miracle on, the cult of the book has become one of the goals and high-priority occupations of students and young couples. The new conscripts of neo-capitalism build themselves altars called bookshelves, or even chapels designated "study," where the book fetish reigns uncontested. [Against this fetishism] the commission of the scientific faculties carried out the ultimate liberating act in regard to the god-book; the tearing up of the books being read in order to distribute segments to each of the members.

Not all the study groups arrived at such a radical critique of bookish praxis. The commission from political science, after having been formed almost exclusively for the purpose of making use of Professor Bobbio, who had declared himself favorable to participating in our commissions, subsequently sank to proposing as its program of study a complete bibliography of the sociologists of conflict. The participation of numerous assistants in this study group is perhaps one of the principal reasons for the backwardness by which, in my opinion, it has been characterized.

The mocking tone—laughter is a principal way of asserting subjectivity—underlines the resoluteness with which the subject arrogates to itself all the decisions in the field of learning and justifies the transfer from general to individual subjectivity. Here too, however, the prevailing contradictions, the strength and weakness of '68, show through: that those who were first in line to destroy the book fetish with the greatest zeal were those who had read and loved books passionately; that the love/hate syndrome concealed the risk of a yielding of the subject's tension, and the eagerness to learn transformed itself into hiding behind social denunciation, into privileging ignorance; that the critique might end in mere destructiveness, the laughter in nihilism toward every culture. Perhaps the opposites were already present, in the weakness of those who wanted to become full-fledged subjects without wholly anticipating the difficulties that such a work entails. The efforts required of an individual in order to create him or herself subjectively and to make a unique and inimitable contribution to a shared subjectivity were overshadowed by the collective elaboration in which the instant of fusion prevailed.

The childish laugh, the genial and refreshing ingenuity embodied two risks—that of retreating into its own opposite, the ossified old man, precisely because it too drastically excluded its opposite, the "*puer*" without the "*senex*"; and that of degenerating into infantilism. The subsequent years offer many examples of the loss of the miraculous equilibrium, the shattering of the spell. But the portents could already be glimpsed at the outset, and paradoxically it was the moderates who saw them, those who feared the excesses and saw only the negatives. However, there was never a totally good period on which evil followed; there was a time in which the tension between opposites was managed adequately, without having to choose definitively between good and evil, between one or the other. The coexistence in '68 of contrary elements was a source of richness, of inspiration, of creativity. It is also the aspect that requires a long while in order to see its good and its evil clearly laid out.

Spaces

One theme emerges as particularly significant in the course of the whole affair: the conquest of a space corresponding to the necessities of the social organization of speech. The old university building offered a structure suitable for discourse among students who had to be able to get together in assemblies and then divide up into committees and groups, accommodating the desire to produce learning, to conduct research, to create culture. For this, numerous halls were necessary, even the dark, ugly ones of the old building; the meeting room in the nearby Camera del Lavoro, offered by the CGIL (Italian General Confederation of Labor, the leftist trade union linked to the Italian Communist Party) when the students were thrown out of Palazzo Campana, was inadequate. Perhaps buildings housing other faculties could have served a similar purpose, but the location of the humanities faculty became an important logistical consideration, since it was right in the center of the city rather than on the peripheral highways or along the Po, like the Polytechnic and many of the science faculties.

Thus, one arrives almost imperceptibly at the symbolic level; and on this level no less than on the concrete level Palazzo Campana became the seat of a privileged communicative space. That explains the stubborn struggle over that space by the students and the academic authorities, the repeated closures and occupations. In the first days the law professors seemed unable to accept their exclusion from the university:

> This morning too [November 29] Professor Grosso, mayor of Turin, did not want to miss his usual appointment and, after having listened to the arguments among the students, managed to "capture" slightly fewer than forty, more or less, for whom he held class in the rector's offices. No other professor came near Palazzo Campana, except the rector, Prof. Allara, who tried to charm the journalists from the various dailies, praising the work of *La Stampa* (which, distorting the facts, attempted to create a "majority" out of motley little groups of monarchists and others nostalgic for the good old days of Fascism) and tweaking the others. (Report by Sesa Tatò in *Unità*, November 30, 1967)

After the initial period, referred to as the big occupation, which lasted from November 27 to December 27, there were many brief occupations broken up by police intervention, requested, as it had been the first time, by Allara, the rector: December 29, 1967; January 10, January 22, February 29, March 1, 1968. On these occasions one witnessed a growing violence on the part of the police, evidenced by reports and photographs in the newspapers. Between one occupation and the next there were periods of shutdown, sometimes lasting several weeks, in which the academic authorities precluded everyone, even themselves, from using the facilities. In addition to the police repression, there were repeated legal denunciations and retaliation at the academic level.

As a consequence of the closures the form of struggle recast itself as a "white occupation," which kept up a presence at the university, disrupting classes but allowing the exam process to take place. The result was an ongoing state of "cultural guerilla warfare," in the course of which the students "disrupted or interrupted university classes and other scientific activities"; in particular the "disruption of one of Professor Allara's classes January 13, 1968, and that of Professor Venturi's February 14, 1968," were recorded. These expressions come from the criminal indictment announced on March 8, 1968, by the Turin City Attorney against 488 students. The crimes included the takeover of Palazzo Campana "carried out along with additional acts directed toward the same criminal plan, in concert with several hundred people, on separate occasions," as well as the use of

> threats for the purpose of forcing the academic Authorities of the University of Turin (Academic Senate–Administrative Council) to revoke the deliberation of the Administrative Council to acquire the "La Mandria" property as headquarters of a [sic] university faculties; to decide to cut short, even temporarily, the didactic activity scheduled for the current academic year; to agree to the demand to oppose the government plan for university reform; to establish for the current academic year and for the future in general, a new curriculum with formats and methods not foreseen by the law, but formulated by themselves.

The crimes variously imputed to the 488 students were amnestied two years later. But in the meantime summonses had been issued, the accused had had to get lawyers and respond to interrogatories. All of this had raised a fuss in the press and, of course, among the families of many of the accused. It was another move in the battle over spaces.

The professors were almost as stubborn as the students in their attempts to reoccupy the contested space; their anxiety may have been even greater. They sometimes seemed to become panicky when con-

fronted with the impossibility of having access to lecture halls and
cathedras they considered their property, places designated for the
transmission of their words to the remaining loyal students. This impelled some teachers to challenge an atmosphere of verbal violence
in order to hold those classes they considered an acquired right. By
depriving them of speech from the cathedra the occupiers had deprived them of an important part of their own identities.

The stubbornness of the students translated into a behavior that,
seen from the outside through the eyes of the mass media, exhibited
almost biological characteristics: the expelled returned, time and
time again, as if to their own habitat, to a home, despite threats and
blows. The building had become the site of a large community, articulated in smaller communities, the seat of live, active human relations. These were not limited to speech, but discourse and its space
were the center of the contest for power, the point of departure and
the fulcrum of liberation.

Guido Viale:
The students would arrive at the assembly and they would tell
everyday experiences, about how the teachers were shits. People
freed themselves, had their say, and lived everyday life in a different way.
The direct confrontations with professors were the best: these students
who told the professor to his face what they thought of him, looking
him in the eye.

From speech to the liberation of bodies, from space for a different
discourse to space for sleeping and eating, living together.

Laura Derossi:
. . . a change in contact, in touching each other. If you go to school in
normal times, someone sits down close to you, touches your leg? right
away you're a little put off. There, you didn't give it a thought. They
could even climb on top of you, hug you, kiss you, it was all totally
normal. The big lecture halls were always overflowing, so you were
really piled in on top of each other. But I don't remember anything annoying, about men with regard to women, attempts to be cute, to be the
big stud, during that period, it was like that type of attitude had suddenly been abolished.

Diego Marconi:
I remember one evening when there was a protest committee, it co-

incided with supper and so you had to set the table there, in a lecture hall. We set the table and someone started singing, and everyone started singing: "Our country is the whole world," and meanwhile they were cooking stuff, dishing out the pasta and it was a very beautiful moment.

From the conquest of a circumscribed space to the hope of liberating a very vast space: the world. The relevant aspect of the space acquired lay in its symbolic force as well. It was a physical space, a structural space, a didactic space, all terms found in the documents of the student movement. But above all, it was a place for freedom of speech, a discursive and communicative space, for the students among themselves and with the outside world.

The occupiers felt the need to invent a "protest newspaper," a mimeographed *Bulletin* that carried news of the goings-on in the occupied faculties, in the secondary institutes, which had also quickly risen up in struggle, news about the protests throughout the province of Turin and the region of Piedmont. The first edition came out January 22, 1968; the paper continued, with some lapses, until May, with a circulation of 1,000 to 3,500 copies.

It is significant that the *Bulletin* included a column called the "Anti-Stampa." In reality, one of the toughest battles that the new speech had to fight in order to carve out for itself a resonant space was against a rather more powerful and older voice, that of the largest daily paper in the city, *La Stampa*. At the time the paper was principally—later wholly—owned by Fiat. Since 1948 the head of *La Stampa* had been Giulio De Benedetti, who had achieved a notable success in increasing circulation, focusing particularly on certain sectors such as local events and domestic news. It was just these columns that had offended the students because of the indignant and slanderous tone in which they depicted the protest. It was another example of an attitude characterized on the cultural level by a narrowness of vision, a conservative provincialism, which Ronchey would only partially begin to modernize when he succeeded De Benedetti in December of 1968.

The two voices were incompatible. *La Stampa,* defender of the social and intellectual order, downplayed and distorted. Like the rector, it considered the occupiers a minority and called for the intervention of the studious majority. In addition to the news reports, it had made use of letters from readers in the column "Mirror of the Times," which had broad, city-wide resonance. In that column letters from worried parents alternated with letters from students with stories of their sacrifices, and with letters from outraged citizens. Finally, the newspaper devoted space to articles by teachers and journalists who attempted to explain the phenomenon of the student revolts with an analysis of youthful "angst" and the backwardness of the university.

Right from the early days the occupying students responded blow for blow:

> we consider it opportune to make it clear that people are not "bivouacking" inside Palazzo Campana, as written in your newspaper, but are carrying out intense didactic activities. (Communiqué reported by *Unità*, November 30, 1967)

From documents to refute an interview with the rector Allara or an article by Professor Grosso defending the freedom to teach (*La Stampa*, December 3, 1968) they went on to the almost daily responses and corrections in the *Bulletin*'s "Anti-Stampa." This paper alternated a serious tone with witticisms, iconoclastic puns, and with denunciations of inaccuracies in information, such as a letter attributed to two women students in the movement in which they complained of the difficulty of studying under the prevailing circumstances. *La Stampa* had to acknowledge the false attribution, but never stopped maintaining that "the majority of students *was* opposed to the disorder." When Alberto Ronchey, sent by the newspaper, introduced himself at an assembly of the Turin movement, he was asked to pay to attend; Ronchey chose to leave.

Given the disparity of the contestants, it was not a matter of a contest to win over public opinion, but of a thorn, a wedge in the existing public sphere, which tended to modify it, enlarging the space in which opinions could freely contend. However, in those circumstances, such a space was polarized, to the extent that it was exceedingly difficult not to take sides either for or against the protest.

The diatribe with *La Stampa* was part of a larger dialogue with the "conformists." The occupying students thought of themselves as an avant-garde, which spoke a new language and was preparing itself to repel the objections of the good family men, whom they viewed with contempt.

> The criticisms that will be hurled at us by parents will, in the majority of cases, be formulated in a language and with a content designed to supplant our discussions and ways of expressing ourselves. This language is quite often the principal instrument of repression on the part

of families. We quite often find ourselves listening to advice of such a type:

1) "NOW THINK ABOUT STUDYING AND GETTING GOOD GRADES." We ask you . . . if you fully realize the effective content of this expression. Translated into other words, it means "Adapt yourself like sheep to the academic structures."

2) "DON'T GET INVOLVED IN POLITICS, LEAVE THAT FOR OTHERS." That is, "Live without asking yourself how they're molding you, where they're fitting you in."

4) "POOR DELUDED CHILD, DO YOU REALLY BELIEVE YOU CAN CHANGE THE WORLD?" Yes, we do . . .

5) "PAY ATTENTION TO US, WE HAVE MORE EXPERIENCE THAN YOU." Let us indeed begin from the premise that your experience was shaped in schools where the black shirt and jackboots were the uniform. It is a fact that we too have had some experiences and will have others. They are and will be different from yours: they must therefore propel us toward behaviors that won't be identical to yours.

This imaginary dialogue (published in the *Bulletin* of February 27, 1968) was part of an ideal exchange of words with "parents," understood as the previous generation, the generation that had grown up under Fascism, and to whom were attributed conformism and apathy. The real parents were often different from these oblique images, even if they might have used the pharisaic language that was repugnant to the protesting students and was singled out as the principal tool of family repression. The oppression went beyond individual physical beings, it was in the discourse spoken *at* rather than *by* them. The idealized type of the "bourgeois," the good family man, was the target of this punch and counterpunch; it was against his figure understood as a compendium of negative values that the new speech wanted to assert its own existence.

Thus we are once again on the symbolic level, which, however, must not be interpreted as totally detached from the concrete. In fact, a characteristic of the new language, for better or worse, seems to be no longer wanting to separate speech from behavior in the confirmation of its own experience and the coherence of its own ideals. The reference to the "real content" of a discourse beneath its appearances goes hand in hand with faith in the capacity of language, in speech that demystifies, translates, clarifies, denounces. And it goes with the claim of a generational difference, against the identity asserted and demanded by "parents": we are different, we speak a different language, we need suitable physical and discursive spaces. The strength

of the students' attitude lies in not considering themselves so different that they fail to initiate a dialogue, however brusque; it is in continuing to talk, to explain, to tell, sometimes like the talking cricket
in *Pinocchio*, consistent with a self-image, cultivated by part of the
movement, as the best and the brightest.

A fleeting equilibrium—one that, as always, contains the seeds
of its own opposite—also establishes itself on the level of relationships with age, with the life cycle. The students affirm the necessity
of no longer being considered "eternal minors," the desire to be
adults while preserving the privileges of the child (the capacity to
tell the truth, to unmask deceits ingenuously) or even a rejection of
the traditional attributes of biological age, in homage to a new concept of what's young and what's old. Perhaps all this is a sign of new
processes of general juvenilization, a product of (and a contribution
to) the constitution of a new age category, between adolescence and
maturity.

In '68 there is a modification of both the usual boundaries between
youth and adult and the concept of the two phases. Initiation is not
renunciation, adulthood is not gravity and pomposity. The rite of
passage is an emotional upheaval, thus differentiated from one person to the next, and it leads to happiness, to laughter, to relief. Also
sometimes just—but it's not insignificant—to being able to express
and communicate a feeling. Paolo Hutter, then a student at the Gio-
berti high school:

> there was something in '68 that allowed me to experience my first seri-
> ous homosexual love relatively peacefully, even if it then took me ten
> years to figure out that I was homosexual. There was a situation in
> which I didn't feel guilty about having fallen in love with this boy, I
> managed to give a name to my feeling and even to talk about it with
> some people—not many.

Peppino Ortoleva:
Until '68 I had been enveloped in one of those typical high school
horror films; I had been in love for years with a girl, who was in love
with another guy, who was in love with yet another girl. When this
girl I loved so much showed a tiny chink in her defenses, I ran as
fast as I could, in other words one of those deals that can't stand
happiness.
For me '68 was this double thing: the discovery of sexuality in general
and the discovery of an emotional relationship with a real person,
with whom I made love for the first time. The first time for both of us.

We went to some friends' house, where I was so moved I set fire to a curtain by accident. It was in that house that, making our way through the accumulated layers of stuff, we consummated our romance, with great joy. It was a very intense love, very mutual, very happy.

In '68 there weren't great unhappy loves. In reality maybe there were, but no one talked openly about them, whereas in the previous adolescent community it was virtually a sort of trademark: "I have an unhappy love, dear sirs, and I'm entitled to be here with you"; afterward, instead, if you had an unhappy love you kept it to yourself. One privilege of the previous adolescent culture, with all its disgusting qualities, had been free access to and respect for depression. There was no room for the depressed in '68.

Laughter and Games

The discursive space that had been conquered came to be defended with the spoken and written word, often with the mocking word, which flowed from spoken to written, rather than shifting the plane of written discourse toward orality. Leaflets and bulletins written in a jocular tone, not always in the best of taste, poked fun at professors and assistants. At times the caricatures in these fliers were quite well done, other times the drawing was so basic that only the caption could explain its significance.

The hidden, the private, the unspoken were exposed through forms of laughter. Irony reassembled the person divided between public and private and attacked individual idiosyncracies. Sarcasm didn't spare even the most democratic and supportive teachers. A good example is a leaflet depicting Professor Quazza divided in two by a line; on the left he's dressed in military style and spouts phrases like "If you were consistent you would take up arms" ("private legal person") while on the right he's dressed in civilian clothes, with expressions like "Excuse me, Miss, but are you confusing the two figures of the medieval merchant!!??" ("public legal person: dean, professor").

The comic quality and the joke even spread to the gestures of protest, intruding on the forms of demonstration and exposing their theatrical nature:

Peppino Ortoleva:
There were very playful moments, like the stunt with the paper flowers. We went into the classes each one of us with a huge paper flower,

totally blocking everything, without having to say anything because everyone was paralyzed looking at the flowers.

Laughter accompanied the moments of verbal violence and constituted a weapon against authority. It is interesting to read this summary of the disruption of a class, which had legal consequences. It took place during an exam period when the students were claiming the right to a concession from the rector permitting them to use the lecture halls from five o'clock to eight o'clock. Professor Venturi, just back from the United States, was supposed to hold class right at five o'clock, but he had found students attending the class who disputed his right to speak, claiming it for themselves, for the "movement."

As soon as one student raises his hand, the professor responds shouting: "You can't ask to speak! Until the class begins no one can ask to speak and *I* am the one to declare the class open."
Thus, everyone awaits the Solemn Declaration of Opening. New request to speak. Shout: "when the class has begun, no one speaks! *I* am the one who gives permission to speak, and I don't give it to you! I demand silence!" An explanation follows: if you want to speak, you can go outside, to Valentino park, no one makes you come to class. For discussion, there are seminars, every Thursday at six.
Subsequently there is an alternation of short discourses on the Enlightenment and new shouts, as soon as someone asks to speak. Shall we pick out the best? Let's choose: "I don't debate with a mob," "the class is not an assembly," "it is *I* who preside over this assembly," "I grant you a single liberty: that of using your right foot and your left foot to leave" (stenographic texts).
Furthermore, Professor Venturi expounds in an agenda written on the blackboard his concept of the class: "Given the incivility of your methods, I ask the [grammatical correction of direct object to indirect object on the suggestion of the Assembly] students to be quiet and I declare that I am the *only* one responsible for order during the class."
After further vocal exhibitions by the Teacher, it is decided to leave him to his Enlightenment thinkers. The Assembly leaves the hall. His wife and six (6) students stay to hear Venturi.

This summary, published in the *Bulletin* of February 16, 1968, circulation 3500 copies, displays a somewhat heavy, almost vulgar tone of ridicule. This tone, recurrent in derisive writings and drawings, arouses disdain even in the memory of some:

Diego Marconi:
these things that were said and done against professors usually
weren't funny at all. They were forms of verbal and graphic aggres-
sion on the part of people who had very little sense of humor.

Nonetheless, the resumption of that mocking tone is indicative precisely because of its tastelessness, because of its coarse guffaw. It re-
proposes in public the crass jokes that students have always made
about their professors, the whispered wisecracks, the notes passed
from desk to desk. That laugh, specifically because of its elemental
nature, wipes out, levels, goes back to the starting point. Patrimony
of generations of frustrated students, it maintains their giggle and
their amusement, infantile and for this reason sharp, irritating, capable of truly annoying the professors. The transition to the public
sphere, by means of the spoken and written word, instills a sense of
liberation, of relief, of power.

For similar exhibitions in other times and places there has been
talk of an updating of popular comic culture, of the lowbrow tradition, of laughter in the piazza and in public. That the deep root may
always be tradition should not be excluded. But here it is possible to
detect direct antecedents: old-fashioned lowbrow humor and a certain "Blues Brothers" type of comedy found in the radio programs for
young people, which, in the sixties, alternated absurd gags and rock
music, as the title of this piece in the *Bulletin* reflects: "The Venturi
Show, or The Howlers from the Cathedra." The result is a translation of the world of academic authority into the everyday language of
the young. Irreverence may be rich or poor, inventive or repetitive,
but it is also valuable as the termination of an attitude of insincere
dependence no longer responding to a deep respect for knowledge
transmitted and its values.

It is not difficult to imagine the reaction of Professor Venturi, anti-
Fascist intellectual and scholar of international renown, to this attitude on the part of the students. One can deduce it from the recollection of a protagonist of those events.

Laura Derossi:
The democratic professors experienced it in a very traumatic way, actually getting to the point of saying very heavy things, like: these are
things the Fascists did, this is the intervention of politics in culture, a
classic of the Fascist system. Because really there was a lot of violence,
we were out of control. Nobody could do anything anymore at the university, whoever did anything was interrupted by hordes of barbarians

who went in with bullhorns explaining why they were disrupting the class: "We want to build our culture for ourselves, science is not objective, rather it's man who determines it, we aren't the ruling class, we want to learn to criticize society and not to submit to it."

The two antagonists, students and democratic professors, both claimed continuity with the Resistance to Fascism, a real struggle over a legacy of values. In the end this gave them a common ground for discussion.

Laura Derossi again:

The police were inside Palazzo Campana, we all go in, Getto was holding class, the hall full of students, guarded by the police outside, with the carabinieri in front of the door as well. At a certain point, Luigi, the heroic one, suddenly manages to catch these carabinieri off guard, gets his hand on the doorknob, goes in, and shouts in a voice full of shock something like: "You can't have class in a hall guarded by the public security forces, this isn't a class, here we're in a military barracks." They grab him, the carabinieri jump all over him—this was the first example of serious violence—and they dragged him down the steps, really dragging him.

In its mixture of claims to space for socially committed speech and of radical mockery, the struggle on the cultural level generated internal contradictions.

Peppino Ortoleva:

This cultural guerilla war was a game, but I don't know how much we all liked it. It was very wearing, it was very frustrating. Because in many many cases the students thought the professor was right. It created violent rifts, when instead we loved unanimity. A mass movement doesn't much like to be contradicted. And so it had its notable moments of risk, of heaviness. In a lot of cases it was a dialogue between the deaf, they weren't there to listen to you, they didn't understand what you were saying.

Once again the student movement revealed its duality, its living in two times and on two levels, that of a circumstantiated revolt and that of an epochal, generational, emotional revolution. A further difficulty of interpretation lies in the fact that in order to oppose itself to the old the movement assumed extreme positions, which, in the course of ten years, would be abandoned.

It is necessary to link the diffusion of obscene, blasphemous, irreverent language to this type of mixture of cultural roots—renewal of student traditions, liberating game, assertion of generational difference and of belonging to the "people." That young people would use many expressions of that type among themselves was nothing new; what was new was that they used them openly, punctuating their remarks in assemblies and their ordinary conversation with sexual terms and curses. It was particularly new for women, for whom it constituted another moment in that emancipation that, passing through the peer group, bore an overwhelmingly masculine stamp. Some women who today have abandoned such language remember the equalizing value it had at the time, compared for example to male companions who—before '68—using it among themselves, hastened to excuse themselves if they used one of the forbidden words in front of a woman.

As a whole this usage was certainly the sign of a liberation of language from its customary norms, of a desecration that, in the cultural context of the end of the sixties, had shocking effects. To shock, to break, to embarrass, these were other forms of cultural guerilla warfare that a part of the movement wanted to practice. Voluntarily or not, they rehashed the proposals of the avant-garde of the twenties, along with their implication of confusing language and reality, symbolic plane and social plane, art and life. The consistency that emerges from similar formulations tends to eliminate the separateness of each of its specific spheres—politics, artistic expression, language—from life.

There was a similar message contained in the proposition of "revolution in daily life" advanced by the situationists in prior years and reinterpreted by Viale and by the hardline wing of the Turin movement. The situationist critique had included the liquidating laugh, the happening, and the *détournement*. Traces of this are also present in Turin '68, even if swallowed up in a growing social commitment. Remarks of situationist inspiration pop up here and there (for example, in the "Documents for the Protest," no. 2, printed in March 1968, sociology is defined as the "self-awareness of the industrialized imbecile"). The *détournement* is very much present in the puns, in the inversion of slogans, in the wisecracks. Situationism, in accordance with its own theoretical formulation, was dissolving into the movement and from a narrow minority affair was passing on to mass dimensions. In this transition its laughter changed in tone too and was not always able to maintain the mordant and mocking edge conferred by isolation.

A Leader

One of the moments when the protest's creativity expressed itself best, expanding into the urban space, was in the context of Guido Viale's imprisonment. Viale had been arrested by two plain-clothed agents on Thursday, April 11, in front of the Fiat Mirafiori plant during a strike over pensions, and he had not been freed on bail. In previous weeks students had been present in front of the factory gates

> primarily to prove to the workers whose side they were on, to make it clear that those of us at the University are not fighting a student battle but the same battle as they; that is, that we are struggling against an unjust society which destines some people from birth to be managers like their fathers and others to toil their whole lives like cogs in a wheel where their labor costs less than the maintenance of a machine. This society cannot understand why someone who has the privilege of tomorrow playing the pimp with respect to the workers renounces it. (*Bulletin*, April 23, 1968)

The student movement reacted forcefully to the imprisonment of its comrade, because of his particular role as well, in which once again the symbolic and concrete levels were interwoven. Viale was actually capable of voicing the most radical demands of the movement, of collecting and expressing the confused destructive aspirations, and not only the theoretical positions but also the values: indignation, argumentative intolerance, toughness, courage, extreme consistency, and the sudden smile. In a movement that had speech at its center, passion for the precision of language was extremely important for a leader.

  Moreover, on a symbolic level there was a complex of factors at work: his physical appearance itself, thin and androgynous, his long, blond hair—in addition to his status as an orphan—all contributed to render him a person who made no concessions to the status quo, somewhere between the legend and the rebel.

Peppino Ortoleva:
Guido had grown his hair out and he was growing a beard and everybody was saying: "But does he really want to look like Jesus Christ?" Then his arrest, the chant: "Guido Viale is the enemy of capital!" He was also legendary because he had been born in Tokyo, he was an orphan, he lived in a garret. But the most important thing was the in-

transigence of his way of reasoning as well as his way of being, which fascinated you. He was the personification of antiauthoritarianism.

Viewed from today, and by laymen, the complex could also represent an interpretation of the local, subalpine character, of a rigor that, in his case, went beyond the rules of good sense and hinted at a shyness, at an inner solitude, at the denial of every indulgence. Other important and fascinating leaders existed in the Turin movement: many interviews speak with admiration and respect of Luigi Bobbio; the women's memories emphasize the strength of the new female image represented by Laura Derossi. But the figure of Viale emerges with a particular symbolic suggestiveness, almost the emblem of a period and of a spirit, a repository of identification, of projections, of restless hopes. All this, of course, in a fashion relatively independent of the actual identity of the individuals named.

Viale himself particularly remembers two aspects of his leading role—the interaction between the ideas worked out during the summer and the subsequent developments:

> the insistence on the everyday aspects of life within the institutions (dissecting in their tiniest details the forms of oppression in which the relationship between student and culture took shape) was a *collective* activity. It's not like I had thought out all these things before: attention to everyday matters was a prior thing, but the content, no . . .

and a commitment without reservations:

> My own notion of how I become a movement leader is that I did a tremendous amount.

But the memory of others, especially of those who belonged to the radical wing of the movement that constituted the majority, clarifies other aspects.

Marco Revelli:
I remember Guido Viale's irreverent energy when we had barricaded the doors of Palazzo Campana and to block them we had used the sacred cathedra of Allara, who had terrorized us the year before. Allara was the type who gave lectures spouting totally idiotic phrases which were only meant to be memorized so at the exam you could give him an impression of whether or not you had been in class. Like, to express the distance between right and morality according to judicial posi-

tivism: "if the legislator decrees that every Friday widows must go out
nude with six funnels on their heads, widows must do this, because
the legislator decrees this." At the exam you had to repeat the example
of the nude widows, otherwise he gave you a really low grade. The
idea that Allara's cathedra had been used as a barricade to shut the
door was something that made me incredibly happy.

And I remember that one day, during the time when Allara should
have been holding his class, Guido Viale was standing on the cathedra,
and Allara showed up behind him, because he had gone through the
cellar, and Guido Viale insulted him, standing with his feet—he had
these huge English shoes—standing on his cathedra, this long-hair, all
the worst things there could be for Allara. He was saying to him: "Get
out of here," using the familiar *tu* with Allara who was using the formal *Lei* saying: "Get down immediately from that cathedra. You are
violating a judicial norm," and he goes: "Shut up, imbecile, you've tormented the students up to now." He put on a show that qualified him
as charismatic leader, and that, for me—I was just a freshman—was an
incredible demystification.

Recollections shed light on the nature of leadership as no other
document does. The informal organizational structure and the state
of emergency favored a charismatic leadership, sometimes defined as
"verbal leadership."

The poles of leadership were Guido and Vittorio [Rieser] as two methods of reasoning: on one side Guido Viale's lucid and crazy extremism,
on the other Vittorio's mediation, his ability to grasp different feelings
that would come out in a meeting, to synthesize them into positions
and to demonstrate the possibilities for mediation and the areas of
conflict. My attitude toward Vittorio was to admire him, to find him
useful and not to love him, while my attitude toward Guido was to admire him, to find him less useful at certain moments, but to love him a
lot more. (Revelli)

These feelings expressed themselves in a protracted verbalization
about the leaders:

I was among the peons, and for us these leaders were fairly charismatic, when we went out we talked a lot about them among ourselves.
Of the leaders, for me, the one I loved most was Guido. Maybe because
he had gotten even with Allara or because he was the most extremist. I
don't know. I remember then when he was freed from prison and he

arrived . . . he had on a heavy reindeer jacket, I remember it. Nothing else, I cared for him a lot. (Revelli)

In this area the movement was homoerotic. It was much easier for men to acknowledge feelings of love for the leaders, who, for the most part, were also men than it was for the women to discover and accept new forms of female authority. There were numerous women in intermediate cadres positions, but very few in leadership positions, and they evoked mixed feelings of envy and emulation in the other women. At the same time, as various accounts confirm, they represented a model that was not wholly desirable because of its implicit rejection of traditional femininity.

Given all the circumstances, it is understandable that Viale's arrest was in various senses, perhaps more symbolically than actually, a serious blow to the movement. The students organized many forms of protest—leafleting, processions, demonstrations that united the theme of Viale's release from prison with that of police repression in Italy and Europe. On April 24 there was a tough march in running phases that lasted for many hours. There had been two leaflets announcing it, one directed at the students, referring to the response of the German students to the attempted assassination of Rudi Dutschke, the other directed at the Fiat workers reminding them of the "joint presence [of students and workers] in front of the factory gates during the past days of struggle."

On Saturday the 27th, when the city center would be most congested, there were demonstrations that reactivated the element of creativity and the theatricality of the jest joined together. The big Standa department stores became theaters for an information and propaganda action:

A hundred or so students, divided in groups, go into Standa. Each group has a specific interventionary task in relation to the location of the various salons-departments and the passageways between the various floors. They engage people directly, trying to start debates. They get into loud conversations in order to provoke a reaction from the customers. Chanting slogans, they improvise short processions that wind among the displays. Of course the police were present in the department store and in some cases they intervened in an intimidating manner. Finally toward five o'clock the management of Standa decided to lower all the shutters except those on some doors.

At the same time other groups improvised demonstrations along Via Roma, in Piazza San Carlo, in Piazza CLN, whether under the porticos

or in the middle of the street. Other groups dramatized the hunt for
Viale, police repression, the climate of paranoia prevailing in Italy currently. (*Bulletin*, May 1, 1968)

Memory has handed down to us the entertainment value of that
form of protest.

Peppino Ortoleva:
Andrea Brero and I were there. I was dressed very nicely, with a jacket,
vest, tie, because I was supposed to play the part of the bourgeois. I
even wore a hat. He was on one side of Via Roma and I on the other.
And in a very loud voice he was saying: "They've arrested Viale," and
I was saying, "Who was Viale?" and he was saying: "He was a student," "Oh, the usual good-for-nothing." People were really dumb-
founded. Then we had some sandwich boards: "Free Viale." At a certain point there was another guy with a "student" sandwich board
who played a dog, and I was there, still dressed like a bourgeois, beat-
ing him over the head with my *La Stampa*. All these little theatrical
groups joined together sort of like a procession and went into Piazza
Castello looking very gloomy and shouting: "Don't listen to us, we're
paid by China."

Quarrels

Turin 1968 has often been viewed as a consentient phenomenon,
especially in contrast with movements in other universities. Those
movements tended to be characterized more by the presence of opposing political groups or line-ups, which also engaged in very
heated debates.

Compared to Rome and Milan, the situation in Turin appears relatively more harmonious; the insistence on themes such as the condition of the student contributed to that harmony. Polemicizing with
the positions sustained by the Milan student movement, Viale asserts:

There is a clear difference between an interpretation of the mass of
students as proletariat and therefore legitimate carriers of subversive
and revolutionary content, and a concept of the students as petty bourgeoisie and potential carriers of dangerous content who require a
guide and have an absolute need to forget the more personal themes
because they run the risk of being antiproletarian. [For us] the revolt
against our own condition in the academic institutions and in the

social environment was a source of political and cultural content adequate to nourish a movement with broad resonance. [We thought] that the proletariat was something very large, which included different social groups, the workers, the unemployed, employees, students.

If such a basic formulation was shared by the majority of the Turin movement, it was still a long way from being unanimously held. It is important to examine some of the quarrels internal to that discursive space, because the same issues reappeared later and still posit themselves today.

In the first place, it's worthwhile remembering that over 600 students had voted for the takeover on November 27, 1967, while about 60, among whom especially the monarchists and Fascists, had voted against it (*Unità*, November 28, 1967). These rightist youths were associated with the Italian University Alliance, "VIVAVERDI" (Viva Vittorio Emanuele Re d'Italia) Group, one of the groupings of the old university politics. Numerous times they forced their way into the occupied university and were thrown out of assemblies and committees. The rector gave them a legitimacy, partly based on the fact that one of their number, Luigi Rossi di Montelera, had until December been president of one of the organs of the old university politics, the Interfaculty.

The students opposed to the protests formed a "Coordinating Committee," which irregularly published a mimeographed newspaper. They recognized in a confused and contradictory manner the legitimate reasons for the protest, but they were opposed to the method of the takeover and they judged unacceptable the Charter of demands "because unrealizable under the current legislation and absurd in substance," as well as "linked to an action of mockery against the constituted authorities."

But the most interesting disagreements were others. The camp favorable to the occupation included those who had been active in Catholic-oriented groups (Intesa, Understanding), socialist, communist, and left-wing socialist (UGI, Italian Goliardic Union) groups, and liberal (AGI, Italian Goliardic Alliance) groups, which, in prior years, had given birth to the so-called representative bodies. Since 1948 assemblies elected by the students, from lists presented by various groups, had existed in all the universities; the assembly represented an executive junta and sent delegates to a central body. Such representative bodies administered funds derived from the fees paid by the students and had representation in the university administrative departments that dealt with fellowships, scholarships, fee waivers, student housing and assistance.

With respect to the management of the university and the organization of curricula, the power of the representative bodies was limited to advisory functions. With respect to the students, the low participation in the elections, which in the mid-sixties was estimated at around 34 percent of those enrolled and 75–80 percent of those attending regularly, diminished the representativeness of these bodies. But their representativeness was limited more than anything else by the nature of their politics, in large part modeled on that of the parties, which reproduced the elements of separateness typical of "adult" politics.

The political groupings that had enlivened the representative bodies dissolved into the movement after the early period, but their legacy was not insignificant; these groups had directed the struggles of the sixties, developed cadres that became movement leaders, contributed to creating bonds of familiarity among the politically active youth (of the 700 who participated in the Turin movement "150 of us knew each other from before," Luigi Bobbio).

The political differentiations did not disappear in the movement; even the positions of the Communist Party, which certainly wasn't a consistent force among the students, were presented (via documents). In Turin there was "a magic moment," as some witnesses define it, when unity and pluralism joined ranks. One symbolic episode became the subject of an authentic oral tradition.

Diego Marconi:
There had been a very large assembly—I think in December of '67—in which the antiprotest camp accused the movement of being a projection of the left-wing parties. Then Carlo Donat Cattin, who was presiding over the assembly, waved his Christian Democratic Party membership card. I remember that I went up to speak, I said: "I've always spoken as a private individual, now I speak as national vice-president of AGI."

The first important disagreement was between the group with liberal and socialist tendencies, which today might be described as moderates or secularists (in large part it was associated with AGI, whose left it constituted), and the group representing the majority of the movement (whose principal leaders were leftists, but which included the Catholics). The assembly of April 18, 1968, signaled a turning away from politics on the part of the moderates; when the votes of the two groups were tallied in this meeting, the moderates received 80 votes more or less, while the majority got around 450. The split had existed right from the beginning, between a line of advanced reformism and one of radical opposition. The very idea of the counter-courses had held different connotations for these two groups: for the first it had an experimental value for later reforming the whole university; for the second it represented a way to open spaces of counter-power in the university, which had to function normally, with a relationship of ongoing tension between the two spaces.

An important common ground was the demand for democracy. But even democratization had different meanings for the different groupings. The point of greatest contention regarded negotiations with the academic authorities and the interpretation of the Charter summarizing the demands of the movement. In one document presented in February by fourteen signers of the secular camp (after the reopening of Palazzo Campana for exams, but under the threat by the Academic Senate to nullify the year for all students), there was a denunciation of the "race to the forefront by those who attributed to the movement the role of 'vanguard' in a generic 'global opposition' to the system," belittling or rejecting negotiations on "specific and concrete objectives." The document maintained that "the growth of the movement doesn't happen by means of cultural acquisition of particularly 'advanced' oppositional content, but through its insertion into new and different structures." It also confirmed the movement's "desire to operate as a political component in the University and therefore not only to agree to, but even to demand authoritatively, on clearly specified conditions, negotiations with the Academic Authorities."

At the root of the two positions lay both different political analyses and different states of mind. The line of radical opposition interpreted the desire of many to live differently.

Marco Revelli:
the line that one can't imagine a reform of the universities without linking it to a transformation of the society, because "you can't make an island of gold in a society of shit," was a source of exhilaration for us: it was a way to overcome the limits of reformism, which, in certain respects, would have meant the end of the protest. Instead, this dimension of a university to reform totally until the society is changed allowed us to imagine a very long process of conflict not subordinated to negotiations. For me these negotiations represented to some extent the

fear that the big party might end with a reformist concession on the part of the university higher-ups.

The party included an accentuation of the collective moment, with elements of fusion realized in the daily routine.

Laura Derossi:
In the evenings, if you were in the occupied faculty, you took turns going to eat and there were places where you knew there would be people. We never lost sight of each other, that's the thing. We were always together in one way or another, whether it was in the occupied university or in the Camera del Lavoro or in the biology building or in the architecture building or at the trattoria or at the PSIUP office, which was on Via Po then. We went around in herds. The individual had disappeared, I didn't have an individual life, I no longer did anything by myself, I didn't read a book, I lived in this herd.
Luigi and I were always together, but always in the middle of five hundred people. When we went out to eat, at a minimum there were ten of us. Say you went out to eat with six people, then it became twenty, then on top of that another fifteen arrived, and made up other tables. Then someone got up, someone else stayed on. There were places we went and we made friends with the waiters, with the owner, and we ate there, we hung out there.

This attitude went beyond the claim of a critical knowledge; the question was always more emphatically of a political and existential nature, where the two aspects tended to mesh:

Luigi Bobbio:
It was an all-encompassing universe, in which the private and the public got mixed up. For us, the thing we hated most in that period was politics as job, the professional politician, who has his hours for the public and his hours for his private life.
Our objective was to put this all back together, and this made the private disappear. But the public was pregnant with private: "because I put myself out there totally, when I do a public action; that is, the public is the expression of my subjectivity, it is my way of being myself."
In the course of that year it became a life choice that many of us did not question, at least for the next ten years. The personal costs went unnoticed, there wasn't a sense of sacrifice, there was the sense of having a great time.

At the other end the group of secularists was experiencing strong contradictions, because its individual members were undergoing a radicalization in their daily lives that reconciled poorly with their moderation on the political level.

Diego Marconi:
'68 for me was an experience of immense frustration of a series of needs. First of all the need to study, that is, I was experiencing this business of doing politics full time as a very great personal sacrifice. And then too really with respect to my need for recreation.
I didn't want to go to meetings all the time, to go to the protest committee all the time, I would have liked to go up in the hills with Betti. And in fact several times we escaped from the protest committee, we would take the car and go up in the hills.

In reality the divergences were greater than the disagreement between two well-defined components of the movement. A confused uneasiness was perceptible, an uncertainty about what to do. Several accounts speak of a sense of the end already present in March-April. The students found themselves facing the question of "how to proceed," "typical of when you begin to understand that the initial impulse is wearing out" (Bobbio).

The negotiations with the Academic Senate proceeded in a tiresome fashion, between new closures, and oscillations on the part of both the movement and the academic authorities. The push toward a critical knowledge was exhausting itself, the limits of the counter-courses had been apparent for some time—not just their incompatibility with the existing programs of study and with the needs of those who had to take their exams for their scholarships, but especially the contradiction inherent in the radical line of "giving to the political-strategic discourse of the movement the goal of cultural work or of theoretical research which the counter-courses were doing."

In March the reorganization of study activity into commissions with titles more emphatically committed to politics ("Social Struggles in Europe," "NATO and Italian Politics," "National Planning and Private Economic Power," "Manipulation of Consensus," "Demystification of Ideologies," "Condition of the Worker in the Affluent Society") accompanied the growing awareness of an unresolved problem:

The greatest difficulty consists in knowing how to direct the cultural work toward a type of political presence that is oppositional not only for its contraposition to the traditional university, but for a methodol-

ogy and content that serve the movement through the individuation of
a strategy and tactic of struggle. (*Bulletin*, March 27, 1968)

In reality, every goal-directed effort presented the danger of be-
traying the original inspiration of unfettered research, of critical
knowledge.

The expansion to the social sphere did not replace that inspiration
in a painless fashion. First and foremost, it involved a change of political personnel.

Anna Trautteur:

Up until the spring I always participated. Then I couldn't identify with
it too much. I had taken part, I had thrown myself into it because I
identified with what the protest was. The things we were protesting
were things I had experienced myself, that I had felt, that I agreed
with. Afterward I had the sense that the university, the student movement, certain demands had decidedly slipped into second place.
They had become more than anything a pretext for another type of
discourse. It's not that I was against that type of attitude, but I didn't
identify with certain, let's call them, ideals. As a university student I
agreed with certain things, with others I didn't see how we could make
any difference. I couldn't define exactly what it was, maybe a too hasty
politicization, a losing sight of certain things. And so I detached myself, even if then I continued to keep up with a lot of things from the
outside, but I no longer took part in the assemblies or anything.

On the other hand, many developed an intolerance for the forms of
extension to the social sphere adopted up to then:

We cannot believe that our action can be limited to holding demonstrations in the city center provoking the "conformists" or causing
anxiety for the good family men who, because of the disrupted traffic,
get home late for dinner. To provoke, to irritate, is not enough: if one
wants to carry out a political action that counts, it is necessary to propose to *organize the social forces that are disposed to struggle.* Soon
we must begin to hold demonstrations in the working-class neighborhoods and in the new developments on the outskirts. (*Bulletin*, April
27, 1968)

There were conflicts regarding the method of moving beyond the
confines of the university. Conjointly with the resumption of strikes
at Fiat in March, one part of the old nucleus of *Quaderni rossi,* led by

Dario and Liliana Lanzardo, proposed to the students a new grouping, the Worker-Student League, which should "make a contribution to the class struggle." Even the student revolt presented itself in that vision as "acquisition of class consciousness" and on this basis could propose for itself a direct intervention at the factories.

The operation devised by the student leaders, on the other hand, was to reach the working class through a long process of concentric circles, initiated by those closest to their targets: from the scientific faculties and the Polytech to the intellectual associations of journalists, doctors, lawyers; from the pre-university students to the evening students, point of contact with the working class, which would finally be reached after having been circled.

Vittorio Rieser, then an assistant, held an intermediate position in that debate; while recognizing the "ambiguous class position of the students" he emphasized the "very strong interest of the workers in the student struggles" and the "enormous possibilities for communication (leaflets, newspapers, discussions) and for common action (leaflets, student picketing at strikes, worker participation in student demonstrations)," which created openings for a relationship between workers and students (from a document presented by Rieser in March 1968).

In the meantime the repression become more pronounced, much of the leadership was arrested and then released, the sense of emergency was growing. The requirement of democracy diminished due to internal and external difficulties, plurality of opinion did not seem a precious commodity. Even the Catholics who had stayed with the left were no longer Christian Democrats; they had been radicalized. The prevalent state of mind was intransigence: "we were all infinitely more moralistic than we are today" (Marconi); "very convinced of not having to mediate, of shooting straight" (Bobbio).

On the other hand, the triumphant atmosphere of the French May was on its way, the new and broader communication among social strata, foreseen in Turin in March. Tuesday, April 30, the *Bulletin* came out with the headline: "For the first time throughout Europe students will march with workers on May 1."

In fact, one could say that it was a historic date. In the course of half a century, the shift in character of the student protests, from an interventionist and nationalistic tone to the demand for social justice and rejection of their own class privileges, could not have been clearer. It carried with it hopes of social regeneration springing from something other than critical knowledge and concealing the desire for even bigger discursive spaces, for words that would break down

social barriers. A further and more drastic annihilation, a resurrec-
tion unspoken but strongly perceived. It might be interesting to hear
it expressed by someone who did not share it, such as Diego Marconi:

> We were a generation of studious achievers. And opposite this human
> material there was the mass of desperate people, of those who were
> doing really badly in school, partly because they didn't study, because
> they were ill-suited, because they were pissed off at the professor. The
> "Chinese"—that's what we called the dominant majority line then—
> took this mass of misfits who came straight out of the dismal fifties and
> made political militants out of them, of various types of course, but
> people who had an identity, values. An enormous and admirable
> work, a channel for maturation and redemption for hundreds of peo-
> ple. At the time I was very shocked by the fact, it seemed to me a very
> Dostoevski-like operation.

The university issues ceased to hold interest before this type of involvement of a political generation: "after the French May we were
ready for anything" (Peppino Ortoleva).

In the meantime the head of the Teachers' College, Professor Guido
Quazza, who had disassociated himself a number of times from the
positions of the Academic Senate and had always had an attitude of
openness toward the students, reached a separate accord, agreeing to
seminars, group exams, important modifications in the organization
of studies. The Academic Senate made many concessions; for better
or worse the academic year was saved.

In subsequent years the student movement continued to exercise
an influence on university structures, in a contradictory fashion. But
the tide of revolt had turned, the *movement* had moved elsewhere.

Luigi Bobbio
In the 1968–69 academic year there was nothing left, there were
groups, but the movement was no longer there. At the same time instead it happened that the workers' struggles moved ahead. And then
there was a sort of attraction, the thing that we wanted to avoid happened. The pole shifted there. And then, after the collapse of the
movement in the university, it was as if the movement had produced
militants who didn't know what to do. By now, their private life was
politics and they had to apply it to something, but they had lost the
objective. For me the period between '68 and '69 was very painful because we couldn't do anything but political militancy, yet we couldn't
do that, because everything we did slipped through our hands. At a

certain point we wound up applying this desire to Fiat. And then a year later we, all of us, did what Lanzardo had told us we'd do, even if in a different fashion. But that's another story.

The real innovation of the Turin movement had been the discovery of new subjects, which established themselves with their own social conditions as their starting point:

Guido Viale:
We were convinced that the students as students were a subject as such. The theory that justified this, which we sort of invented and sort of took from Rudi Dutschke, was the discourse on institutions: the institutions are depersonalizing and authoritarian and the fact of belonging to the institutions gives you the status to rebel against them. It was important to say: "Everyone stakes his own experience in the struggle. I rebel against my oppression, not against that of the Vietnamese. I am with them because we are struggling against the same enemy, but with respect to the problem of my liberation—I am the student as student. My enemies are the academic authorities, the rituals of the university, the authoritarian culture and cultural manipulation. For the workers, it will be something else, something different. Perhaps they are more important than us, count for more, but our speaking out as individual testimony is worth as much as theirs, because it is a testimony of liberation.

With the exception of a few locations, such as Trent, these were totally isolated positions within the national student movement. To appreciate the isolation it is sufficient to hear the reasons that one of the most sensitive Roman leaders, Franco Russo, gives today to explain his judgment that the Roman movement was "more radical":

Rome started later, but started more radical, with many politicized cadres, and it quickly involved thousands of people. The question of expanding our sociopolitical sphere confronted us immediately; the movement quickly adopted an anti-imperialist tactic. It wasn't something born just of university issues. Rather, I would say that that was a subsequent and imitative thing, even if we did the counter-courses, disruption of classes, one-person-one-vote, you're familiar with these things.

Luigi Bobbio again:
We were very much misunderstood, by the Milanese, very much so by

the Romans. And we were really pissed off at them, there was a very
strong conflict.

We explained to them for example the importance of the struggle against the professors—we attributed great importance to this point, as a liberating element, of liberation from authority. And they said: "But these are absurdities. The professors aren't important. Sure, you can do it, but we should be fighting against capital, we must find a relationship with the working class." In the abstract, because, after all, in Rome there weren't even any workers. I remember debates, nights spent arguing with the Romans, I would say to them: "But in Rome you don't have any workers, what do you care? In Rome you have the employees of the ministries, it's a city made up of government employees, there aren't workers, you should be talking with the employees of the ministries." Naturally they weren't the least bit interested. They didn't see the internal element of liberation.

There was really a horror, in that period, of holding oneself out as a vanguard, of creating a party, of saying: "We should direct the struggle of others"; a key word was "communication," of the movement or of the praxis.

Another word very much in vogue was "unilateralness": not posing general problems, but posing them from my point of view. One point of view is always partial, but it's true if it's partial. If it were to become general, it would no longer be true.

Here lies one of the reasons for the current interest in Turin '68 and, more generally, in a certain thread present in all the '68s, independent of their outcomes. One movement in particular could, if it wanted to, call itself the heir to '68: the women's movement and, especially, certain of its radical wings. But this raises a complicated historiographical problem, which we must defer, regarding the relationship between the movements of '68 and the women's movements. Here we can only mention a dissension within the Turin student movement, not expressed then and subsequently spoken of seldom and with difficulty.

The Gender Gap

All the women who spoke to me attribute an explosive emancipatory value to their participation in the student movement. Those who had already been politically and culturally active (in the university, in the parties, working on magazines) underscore the difference of the new experience, in which women were much more numerous and counted for more. This was true particularly in situations like that of the Teachers' College, a faculty with a predominantly female population, where the movement, which was very strong, was led entirely by women. More generally, a pertinent fact is the percentage of women among the 488 individuals indicted in March 1968: 34 percent, a very high number compared to the normal proportion of female participation in traditional politics in Italy, from 7 to 18 percent.

The cause lay in the very form of the new politics, tied to the everyday, to subjectivity, less separated from life. We might add that, if women are acknowledged as being important in all the emergency situations, a state of "simulated warfare" (Franca Balsamo) lent itself especially well to a type of participation in which the symbolic characteristics of ritual and of play were accentuated.

Eleonora Ortoleva's observation takes a similar tack, that women were in the front line of a great theatrical performance:

we were actors and we had a big audience. We were on stage and the others, even those of our own generation, were watching us.

The theatrical game, the ability to divide oneself in two and observe oneself, is part of the formation of subjects. But what internal images guided the women in this appearance before the footlights? One strong impulse was negative: to distance themselves from their mothers, to reject their model completely. The new models offered by the most visible movement women were mediated by an idea of liberation that was partly masculine, partly androgynous. This latter evolved primarily through the peer groups, the groups of adolescents who get together to affirm a diversity as offspring, a group in which age difference prevails over gender difference.

On the other hand, a male model does not mean pure and simple imitation of the male. Traditionally, one example of a liberated woman was the tomboy, short-haired and energetic, a certain aggressiveness in her habits, which she might bring up to date by wearing a miniskirt or pants all the time. Thus, the point of reference was a hybrid, to which one can ascribe the emergence of previously cryptic behaviors, such as smoking and a certain way of smoking, in public and using gestures not customary for women. Maria Teresa Fenoglio remembers her shock at the gestures of the liberated movement women: keeping a lighter in their purses, flicking ashes on the ground, sitting on tables.

The image of the new woman—in a position of power and capable of challenging the traditional rules of female modesty—belongs to the same genre. This image had struck Maria Teresa when she first came into the movement:

> I saw Laura Derossi for the first time and she made an enormous impression on me because she had these really short skirts and you could see her garters. It seemed to me that she was very daring. Then, in order to start a conversation with her, I went: "Psst, your stockings and panties are showing," and she said: "Oh!" and she smoothed her skirt down, but it was like she was doing me a favor, in reality she knew perfectly well.

We can understand that for many women this model was not attractive and they preferred, when possible, to turn elsewhere, to figures of female power such as those offered by English culture (Vicki Franzinetti), with its literary and social heritage.

Many women remember having experienced in '68 a sense of freedom that gave vent to their desire for affirmation and for a public presence. In reality, the women who counted at the highest levels of leadership numbered very few—Laura Derossi for the radical wing, Betti Benenati for the secular pole. They were distinguished by their ability to participate in the general assemblies:

Laura Derossi:
The hardest thing was speaking in the great hall, overflowing with more than five hundred students, and making a speech from the cathedra. Even the men, there weren't many who could do it.

For these women the movement had represented the place of value, which granted an equality denied in the outside world. Laura Derossi remembers that in the early months of the occupation she was spared being arrested because of her sex: "the carabinieri didn't want me, because I was a woman"; that subsequently, in March, she had to insist in order to be arrested with the others accused, and that only while she was a fugitive prior to her arrest, in Milan, in the course of contacts with other leaders from Milan and Rome, did she begin to feel discriminated against:

> My equality ended with the movement. In the movement I had never for an instant had the sensation of being different, of having fewer rights, of being able to do less, never; from then on, always. If they had to choose who would do a document, who would speak, it was automatic that it wouldn't be me.

The form of liberation through politics was very ambiguous:

Maria Teresa Fenoglio:
In reality, I was very intimidated. I puffed myself up a lot—in fact, every once in a while I ask how people remember me and they remember me as a person who harangued the assemblies very forcefully and decisively. Inside, I felt very insecure, but I wasn't aware of it.

This last observation indicates why it is so difficult today to analyze a situation in which gender difference was not experienced in a conscious fashion. The transition from then to now is often defined as from blindness to sight:

Laura Derossi:
I had been quite impressed at having found a woman as head of the student bodies in Berlin. When I saw her again in 1977–78, she didn't recognize me: "See," she herself said, "even I was wearing blinders then, because Luigi I remember, you, no."

The current evaluations, through memory's reflection, separate along two major lines, undoubtedly on the basis of differences in individual experience as well. All the women recognize the elements of oppression present in that liberation, but some emphasize the liberating side. The most touching observations are those on the transition from tormented and depressed isolation to feeling themselves part of a whole, to communication and appropriation of new times and spaces, like the evenings and the city as well as the university. For some women the networks of relationships established then, in Turin and other cities, are still valuable today.

Other accounts stress the aspects of oppression, but especially of self-oppression. This is one of the most striking differences from the accounts of the experiences of women in the student movement collected in '76 and published in *Ombre rosse*. Almost ten years later the recollection was still so unpleasant as to impose on all the anonymity of pseudonyms.

"Chiara":
the majority of women, even if students, had a minimally active role in what was going on. The only one who protested and talked was C. and I dreamed several times that she was drowning and I let her drown, smirking.

relationships with other women were substantially nonexistent, in the best of cases, especially with those who "counted" then, who had created their own political space for themselves. They looked through me, as if I were an empty space, or they handed me leaflets to mimeograph, as if I were a mimeo machine, and they made me suffer, I detested some of them.

Not looking at other women, detesting them, wishing for their deaths, as transitional steps of liberation. Perhaps not always obligatory, but historically it happened this way, at least for some women. It is particularly painful, because those transitions involve not seeing a part of themselves, hating themselves, annihilating themselves. They entail a self-destruction that can become a premise of rebirth, but that can also remain a long while as a disintegration, a loss, a shortcoming more serious than any observed in their own mothers.

In the current accounts recrimination and rancor, which held sway back there, are hardly present. There is an awareness of the price paid and of their own complicity in the choices made. Time and the expansion of female intellectuality have permitted an initial historicization.

One of the saddest issues is sexual liberation, a process among the most ambivalent because of how it came about in those years. It contained, at one and the same time, innovation and continuity, a break with taboos and a resumption of old customs that had always made sex a medium of exchange and instrument of communication. But the sexual relationship taken for granted, exercised with some detachment from the emotions customarily attributed to it, integrated itself into the theme of knowledge, of the new learning. Thus, the new terms specific to a Nietzschean "gay science"—curiosity and delusion, experimentation, discovery—are ascribed to the new willingness of women regarding sex, at least when sex wasn't demanded as the price of admission to a clique. For some women it was primarily a matter of a discovery of emotions through the body, from sensuality and falling in love to maternity (Laura Cima). In reality the movement of '68, once again contradictory, legitimated in its extensions that which it denied internally, like female physicality and maternity.

Out of all that came break-ups of monogamous relationships, the formation of new couples, pretensions of open relationships, with the load of grief and happiness and frustrations that they carry. Hence rifts with birth families and new ambiguities between the masculine and feminine poles as well:

'Sixty-eight for me was a continuation of paternal choices, even if I fell out with my father. But the falling-out was on the sexual level, after my father read some of my letters in which it was clear that I was making love not only with my fiancé, but also with another guy.

Nineteen sixty-eight had posited the problem of women's liberation in a more urgent mode than before. This was its contribution. It was impossible to turn back, either from emancipation or from the new forms of oppression. The field of relationships among women was completely open, because the student movement had often kindled rivalries, jealousies, envies. But it had also highlighted the differences among women, something which is always a basis for subjectivity-raising. What remained unresolved was the big problem of love and respect among them:

Maria Teresa Fenoglio:
I wanted to have a positive female figure, because I had this tragedy inside, of not being able to find some important female point of reference, that might somehow give me peace.

Years had to pass before this desire made itself explicit and operative. The adventures of the feminine in our world pass through poverty and loneliness; they include terrible trials, all the more terrible when accompanied by a political and productive commitment, when accompanied by the conviction of doing something right and useful for others.

5

The End of the World

In England again. Eric wants to show me the land of his ancestors. We walk in the freezing wind along a deeply eroded coast on the turbulent sea, green yellow and periwinkle, streaked with white, the North Sea with seagulls flying overhead. Eric tells stories about his grandfather—whose name he bears—who set out from the hills of Norfolk to start a farm in South Rhodesia. His son had moved the farm to South Africa, where there were greater opportunities for study and for work. Thus Eric had grown up on the *veld*, on the big farm run by his restless mother, who lamented her European culture, Venice, and classical Greece.

I ask him to repeat for me other stories that I already know, the ones about his adolescence in Johannesburg—Joburg, he says—the university, the clandestine political struggle, prison, his flight into exile. Eric says he feels constantly in exile, neither English, nor European, nor African, and for this reason he continues to travel without respite, working as a consultant for developing countries that he doesn't believe will ever develop. I too have often felt I was in exile. "But you have Italy," Eric says. I have never considered Italy a resource, but perhaps I am beginning to understand.

(At times, in years past, landing at the Turin airport at Caselle, which seems like the railroad station of a provincial city, I was struck by the green military men with their short machine guns pointed, their puffed pants tucked into their high narrow boots, their slanted berets, and that I-don't-give-a-shit look. It seemed as if I were arriving in a third world country, I read it in the eyes of my neighbors in line at the passport control desks, skeptical and patient eyes from the heights of long-established democracies: "Southern Europe, I like it so well, the people are marvelous." Mediterranean faces of the policemen, seen through those eyes. And yet, for better or worse, they were our bulwarks against terrorism.)

I would also like to understand from Eric why ours has remained a friendship between two vagabonds, without ever becoming a more committed relationship. He listens incredulously to my summary of my affair with X: "you?" and he reminds me of when he came to visit me in '69 during his move from Africa to England: maybe it was possible then, but I didn't accompany him back to London as he proposed, because I was spending all my time in front of the Fiat plant.

After returning from Africa I had lived in Rome briefly, still uncertain whether to stay in Italy or to leave again. Then I had gone to Turin, as a guest of Eble, a childhood friend, who had taken me to the night meetings at the Molinette Hospital. I had quickly been swept up in the swirling river of the worker-student revolt. Thus, in May 1969 I found myself, without any specific political affiliation, in front of Mirafiori, along with many others, handing out leaflets, having after-shift meetings, following the rhythm of the big factory showing up at dawn, at midday, in the evening. I was there mostly to listen—I didn't know anything about it— but full time.

In front of the gates of the Fiat plant—maybe it was Gate 0 of the autobody shop—one of the very first mornings I went, a very cold dawn, Adriano Sofri, leader of Lotta Continua (Ceaseless Struggle), said to me, with a certain sympathy at seeing me shiver: "You're cold, eh?" Now I think it was not only because of the cold; it was also the emotion of seeing rules and social barriers, which seemed insurmountable, overcome.

The Fiat plant functioned as a great magnet from which we couldn't detach ourselves, like iron dust glued to the giant. The dialogues with the youths who came out of the gates transmitted a sense of urgent, immediate transformation in process. They skipped—it seemed to me—the mediations that I had experienced between the white intellectual and the front lines of a struggle for black liberation. I believed I could perceive that we were infinitely closer to a revolution than had ever happened in Africa. Because here we were in the heart of power, and every least thing that happened in the shops came to be fitted into the context of a relationship with power. Thus existence suddenly became meaningful, full of sense, in a direct conflict where people put themselves at risk. We read the newspapers with the state of mind of someone involved in everything that's happening: they were talking about us, because the whole world was watching us.

Once again, I was starting from zero. My money was almost gone, what I had left would last, with some loans, for a few months. I was living with the friend who had taken me in, sleeping on a straw mattress on the floor. As furnishings, once again only chairs. Otherwise the room was totally bare. We always ate out, often sandwiches, other times in the trattorias frequented by the movement.

In my free moments I continued to work on Africa, to finish up the book on Mozambique, which my comrades in Frelimo were awaiting. But when it was published, my primary commitment was something else. Africa had become an object of study, something to which I could devote articles, seminars, and lectures, no longer an all-encompassing commitment.

Once again I had the illusion of finding a country and a role, of no longer being foreign, raving, obscure, of tumbling into the light of history and its mutations. Serve an idea, a movement. Gather the news of the struggle, write it up in the leaflet, give it back by circulating it. Link, transmit, act as passageway, be the vehicle. The PCI workers at the gates of the engine works watched us skeptically. The looks we exchanged with other workers were heavy with reciprocal expectations, with an understanding not fully articulated, with trepidation for what might happen. An intense flow of nonverbal communication continued, over and above the information dispersed about what had happened that day in one department.

I experienced a sense of the end of the world, a mental state of emergency, like an inner perception of an imminent end, with the urgency to act before it was too late. The rhythm of daily life accelerated in order to live up to the circumstances, absorbed in the approach of the eschaton, which might be a triumphant outcome or a catastrophic result. Time curled like a wave repelled by a dike, life was marked by continual deadlines; but what was supposed to fall due? The final hour, the encounter between our time and the time of the definitive uprising of the downtrodden masses.

I wasn't in possession of myself, I was advancing in enemy territory, forced on the attack in the absence of a fixed place in which to come face to face with myself. Perhaps at the time I would not have been able to bear the confrontation. Somewhat entranced gaze, disheveled clothes, from not much sleep and hard work as well, to be sure, but primarily from the permanent state of alarm which demanded that one never stop going.

Many of these sensations became compressed the day of July 3, 1969, with moments of joy, release, relief. The Worker-Student Assembly had called for an unauthorized march for that day, at the same time as a rent strike proclaimed by the union. The scope was identical: extend the struggle from the factory to the working-class districts. I found myself in the front ranks of the march, on Corso Traiano, where phalanxes of comrades with banners and flags were advancing. We could see the police looming black ahead of us. The clash dispersed us among the big blocks of buildings, whose endless stairways offered precarious refuges. We reformed in small groups that made their way through the city, which was without public transportation that day. We traversed the whole city, anxiously searching for our scattered comrades, finding some in a pitiful state from running and from the battle. I had fled, but others had resisted and counterattacked. At the architecture faculty there was a sort of bivouac on our own territory, kept under watch by the police. With their full-page photographs, the next day's newspapers confirmed our impression that we were shaking up the system of power. The sense of community, of sharing a destiny that lay in these things, was very high: things were in movement and we were in the movement, which was carrying us with it. We felt as if we had been hurled, sometimes almost unknowingly or partially knowingly, into a bigger game.

For several days we had been playing host in our bare house to Alfonso, who had been Balestrini's model for the protagonist of Vogliamo tutto. He too embodied, it seemed to me, the acceptance of something that the individual could agree to push to the maximum; but the extremism was already there in the process, which laid bare one's own condition, which rendered unacceptable conditions tolerated up until yesterday, which made extraordinary things seem obvious. The impression was that no one, of the many intellectuals who descended on Turin from everywhere, really understood what was happening. Yes, there was a leadership, divided by divergences in its political line and in its interpretation of the historical phase, that called the shots on a day to day basis. But it too seemed like a cork carried on the waves. I had admired Guido Viale, who, in a tense and important meeting, succeeded in expressing that state of mind, while in general the tendency to appear sure of oneself, to change position without batting an eye prevailed.

When it came to the schism in the fall between Lotta Continua and Potere Operaio (Workers' Power), in an ugly meeting at the headquarters in Via Passo Buole—a big, freezing room, with an inadequate stove—those of us who did not identify with either of the two groups scattered once again. But the community continued to exist informally, friends, comrades, small groups that came together at times. For those who lived in that environment and breathed the air of the movement, loneliness no longer existed.

Continual, obsessive, fascinating political discussions, sense of always and only moving among comrades. Even if we ended up in a new place, with people we didn't know, we were likely to hear someone say to us:

"But you all are in the movement? Right, it's obvious." Maybe the way of dressing too: the gabardine suits, the black capes, the brightly colored African fabrics forgotten, now the uniform was pants and parka. My parka was white, I couldn't stand the military olive drab with the indispensable red scarf.

I see G. again after the Christmas holidays. The silence from which we start off each time and which leavens in the interstices of our discourses is also symbolic of the distance between us.
We talk about how love may include distance; about creating distance without resorting to coyness, subterfuges, tricks, violence.
Not identify with distance, keep one's distance from distance.

Dream: I am on a rock and I look for supports in the overhanging rock in order to climb up. But crumbling stones and dirt remain in my hands. There is no possible support. Inside I am aware of a feeling of powerlessness, I stay curled up on the rock. Looking down, I see the dry earth with blackberry bushes. It seems impossible to me to venture downward either.
G.: a transition where you don't see the destination.
I feel myself in mid-course and the old is no longer okay but neither is the new yet okay. Insist on this place of transition, stubbornly, without wanting to leave it too soon.

X is sick, bad flu. Shut up in his house, an aid system activated that doesn't include me, what remains is only the execrable link via the telephone.
I complain once again to G. Implacable, he cuts short all my efforts to blame others, external things and people. He forces me to bring everything back to myself, insisting that I dissolve the external into internal. It's the ana-lysis, the lysis.

FEBRUARY

Heavy snow, traffic emergency. Unexpectedly X, who had a car with chains, came to pick me up and take me to G.'s office. In the waiting room I felt that gesture of help that lodged inside of me and provoked reactions: admit that someone else might make a "sacrifice" for me, accept the offer.
After I entered G.'s office, I began to voice these thoughts, without know-

ing where the discourse was going. It was like the swift course of the flame along a fuse. Fulminous and incandescent images followed one another:

my father who asks to be pardoned for having disturbed me to go with him when he was sick

my father who has to be taken to the hospital when we are together at the sea and I, a little child, ask him for some money for ice cream and only when he comes back after several days do I burst into copious tears that give vent to my suppressed grief

my father who is about to have an operation and I cannot obtain the plasma for the transfusion, in accordance with the absurd demand of the hospital ("go for a minute to the Molinette Hospital and have them give it to you")

my father who dies and I arrive at his bedside when he has just expired. The images and the words brought me to an abyss—I felt a bundle of muscles between my stomach and abdomen relax and contract. Spasms, shaking, and sobs. Never made such a scene in front of G.

A gesture of devotion unloosed unstoppable waves. Hearing oneself asked for forgiveness by a person one loves had been the sign for me that the relationship between my father and me did not flow with the intimacy and the simplicity that are possible when each person responds to the needs of the other. With him I had been late, embarrassed, incompetent; not efficient, diligent, punctual as I was in my political and professional work. Things too painful to remember and to say.

With G. it's possible. Maybe knowing that he too has a daughter makes me feel that he can share this. G. observes that there are relationships that go beyond the separateness of bodies. Beyond death, which can't conquer them.

Loss, depression, collapse, after the outburst of tears and the feverish days spent with the image of my father. I begin to understand that depression is necessary in order to get to the bottom and fish something out, something at times too heavy. And it's very different from torment.

X gives me orchids and mimosas.

Dream: the conductor on the train calculates that I have had five to six thousand dreams. But in reality, he says, it would be far more, from thirty to eighty thousand.

I dream about having hair on my chest, under a violet jacket. G. takes the opportunity to tell me our relationship lacks hair, aggressiveness. I acknowledge that it is idyllic, but the possibility of a conflict with him scares me. Vicious circle: it annoys me that he disapproves of me because I don't dare incur his disapproval.

I say to G., after a silence, that I'd rather sit on the floor than in a chair, if good manners didn't prohibit it. Because I am "floored," I don't even have a dream to recount, I am too tired. I want to stop myself, I worry about the effect this could have on him.
"Why don't you relax a little, instead of immediately worrying about me?"
"But maybe now I can also begin to worry about you."
Okay, G. says, but the point is the idea of happiness. He quotes Rilke:

> the hanging catkins
> of the bare hazel-nuts, or else
> the rain that falls on the dark earth in spring

to tell me that happiness may be a fall to earth rather than an ascent. And that vice versa sitting down on the ground can be not negative.
Silence.
Now G. wants to know what images are whirring in my head. One: a seagull that hits the water with its big wings spread and suddenly, amidst ruffled confusion, changes into a peaceful little goose. Difficult transition, from motion to stillness, from the air to the water folding those long wings carefully. There springs to mind how much force an airplane must employ to come to a stop when it lands, you feel the braking throughout your body. G. observes that seagulls don't need solid ground, they rest bobbing on the waves. The continual game of double meanings reminds me of my class in high school: we were always on the alert, with our ears open to catch them, and always with a fixed point of reference: love, sex, obscenity. Every word could have such an allusion. G. comes out with one of his remarks:
"And how does the water feel on your seagull feet?"
I laugh: "A bit cold."
"A bit cold," he nods, "it's not yet March."
I don't pursue and I am not pursued, at least for one day.

MARCH

Time stretched out. Weeks as if they were months, the two Sundays so very far apart from one another.
I wrote to an English friend about my tiredness. His concern and the simi-

larity of experiences in his response strike me; he recalls having experienced, years ago, "an exhilarating and anxiety-provoking process, which leads to flexing, that light but distinct movement of the emotions, as if one could feel the 'muscles' of the emotions relax after the strenuous exercise of analysis." Perfect. The muscle relaxes after the long race, the tension subsides. Could the muscle be the heart? These days it is silent, there is no effort.

Tomorrow I will start running again. Now I have time for my memories.

At the end of '69 the massacre at Piazza Fontana in Milan confirmed the emergency for us. It seemed evident that it was essential to transform the movement into an organization, in order to position ourselves to oppose the enemy's plots. The organizational forms had to be flexible, decentralized, inspired by direct democracy. Like many others, a small group of comrades and I—we had rediscovered the youths from the piazza—formed a collective, which planned to engage in agitation in working-class neighborhoods and in factories and, contemporaneously, in the study of Italian socioeconomic reality and the development of political personnel. This last demand was pressing, based on the hope of understanding and "becoming competent." The sense of a lack of "tools" was obsessive, practically a demand that the less educated comrades made on the intellectuals in the group. Everyone felt a tremendous anxiety to be up to the task from the theoretical point of view as well. In our collective we read and studied a great deal, from the history of the working-class movement to the most recent analyses of imperialism.

These studies and the agitation at the factory had become my main occupations. Having by now exhausted every other resource, I was teaching in the mornings as a substitute in a middle school on the outskirts of Turin, attended by uncontrollable kids. Afternoons and evenings group work. Saturday evenings and some Sundays free.

The atmosphere was one of great possibility, notwithstanding the looming presence of neo-Fascism and repression. The social shuffling continued, with a mobility I had never before experienced: for years, from '69 to '73, I lived on a daily basis with individuals from social classes that, in other circumstances, I would at most have met in passing. Even the choice of forming a new group because we didn't identify with those already existing, which we accused of spontaneitism, workerism, Marxism-Leninism, was a sign of the frenzy of initiatives, of the certainty of having something of our own to say. Everyone brought their closest friends into the group, people's love lives even took place predominantly within the collective. However there were daily contacts with other organizations, both at the sites of our agitations and in meetings, especially among small, informal groups such as ours, at which we compared our lines.

The connections were not just within the same city; everyone felt the necessity of getting away from localism in order to arrive at forms of national association. There were meetings, contacts, bilateral and multi-lateral encounters. I particularly remember the meetings of the "Third Tendency," which wanted to reunite divergent groups from the two poles, spontaneitist-workerist and Marxist-Leninist. Agreement was impossible, because some of those present wanted to form a true party, something which for others, including us, was unthinkable.

Instead, through actual convergences—"a few returnees from Africa and some popular leaders from working-class districts," said Romano Madera—we formed the "Gruppo Gramsci" ("Gramsci Group"), with sections in various Italian cities. The name did not derive from a total agreement with Gramsci's thought, but evoked a specifically Italian tradition, to whose reality we were devoting our analyses. We published them in fairly substantial pamphlets and in a magazine, which also had a historic title, Rassegna comunista, for which another comrade and I held the copyright.

The most wonderful aspect of the adventure was the personal but shared commitment to a grandiose undertaking, a gigantic bet with history.

Later it came to pass that the effort generated rancor and recriminations, against those who never mimeographed or swept out the office, against those who arrived late at meetings, forcing others to lose hours of sleep in order to conclude the meetings. The make-up of the big community of New Left groups, articulated in tribes, clans, and subclans, was such that it ended up creating a certain conformism and moralism: disapproval of habits and styles of clothing—such as a fur jacket—that might rekindle the latent hostility of the workers toward the classes from which we came, or might reveal bourgeois self-indulgences. Many things, like going to the mountains and reading novels, were simply out of the question for lack of time, not to mention for fear of setting back the revolution.

I don't believe we ever used this term among ourselves to refer to the process in progress. It was a visible prospect, even if distant, not an imminent fact. However, its possibility was betting on its imminence. On the other hand, given that we were all fairly young and dominated by a spirit of youth—the oldest might have been thirty—the temporal dimension was expanded. I remember an encounter at the home of a dear friend, now dead, whose intelligence, sharpness, and open-mindedness we all admired. Just for a joke we tried a seance—evening, house in the country, desire for distraction from political discussions—on the suggestion of an occasional guest. Naturally the questions asked concerned the revolu-

tion: "when will it come? where? and in Italy?" (the sense of internationalism was alive, especially in our friend, a bit older than we). The spirit
called up was Frantz Fanon, whom he knew well. And caught up in the
spirit of the game, he began to speak to him in French, as if Fanon were
present: "Dis-moi, Frantz, dis-moi. . . ." The answer had been: in 1984,
perhaps to correspond with Orwell. At the time thirteen-fourteen years
seemed to us a long time, not just in terms of years but also because of
the crazy and desperate commitment involving a murderous struggle
against time. A desire to succeed at all costs, magnifying efforts and
sacrifices.

There was an almost religious spirit—we would never have acknowledged it—in our placing ourselves in the service of the masses. Often we
did extremely boring jobs of an informational nature, like leafleting and
speaking in the working-class neighborhoods—at the Saturday markets—
about rents, services, and the concrete possibilities for struggle that might
open up in that area. The group's center was open for consultation on
household problems, because we were certain that we could relate the
smallest contradictions of a material nature to the political organization.
In this respect we were imbued with our Maoist heritage; we had been
much impressed and convinced by the slogan of a group from Trent that
had carried out a campaign over incinerators: "Through trash to politics."
In our area there were rats, and we thought seriously of using them as a
point of departure.

One task that required particular effort, but that we considered a revolutionary obligation, was a knowledge of the organization of labor in the
factories where we were agitating, and also of the pay scale. I remember
cadres-schools in which for once I was in the group that was supposed to
be learning, but I couldn't understand anything about the pay scale. I was
afraid that some worker coming out of the factory might ask me something about it, as occasionally happened, and I would fall short in my role
as leader. Fortunately it never happened.

At the time I was living through a very contradictory phase. I continued to
teach, going from one middle school to another and finally to a preparatory institute for elementary school teachers in Pinerolo. I traveled in my
sleep and in the fog in an old car that constantly lost its muffler, and I arrived as fast as I could at the factory gates, at the central shift change of
the day. I located my comrades with their packages of leaflets ready and I
entered into the discussions. I was still living with Eble, who belonged to
the same group, but then the house was full of furniture that a friend who
had moved to Rome didn't know where to leave. We had gone from one
extreme to the other, with a complete and rather overcrowded household. It included a battery of pots and cooking equipment we hardly
used, from which I still have a few pieces.

I did a great many things in the group, I was part of all the leadership bodies, at the national level as well, executive councils, directives, committees. I often dealt with the inter-groups, a meeting where each group had its representative and which was supposed to decide on common initiatives. I remember exhausting negotiations over demonstrations: banners, slogans, routes, and positions in the processions. These were also the decisions where a hovering problem was posed, but, in general, was barely discussed: violence. This was primarily a matter of defense and discipline, of the traditional functions of the law-enforcement services. At a certain point more serious questions came up, after some bloody experiences with being trapped in mobs. I remember one meeting, probably in '72, where someone said: "Are we always going to take it, why don't we see if we can't be better armed, carry with us not just lemon for the tear-gas, but also something like a molotov cocktail?" and the answer of some comrades was, "It's okay with me, I've got nothing to lose," because the disillusionment, the weariness were already immense, we felt more and more defenseless, disorganized, endangered.

However, the problem had often arisen of whether or not to accept the battle, whether to seek it out, how to provide escape routes. In various cases some leaders had insisted on the importance of bringing people into a clash with the police, especially the students, in order to politicize them. This cynicism entered into the general framework of a mentality that considered violence a given of the capitalist system. The diffuse violence exercised by the state, from institutions, from factories, in addition to the specialized violence of neo-Fascism predominated in our minds. Our violence seemed to us merely a response.

For us the idea of violence—I'm not talking about its exercise—was acceptable on another level as well: our heroes, from the anti-Fascist Resistance to the third world revolutionaries, had made use of it, and precisely on this point they distinguished themselves from the moderates. Not only: we took for granted that sooner or later it would be necessary to resort to violence, as the history of all revolutions taught. We realized that, notwithstanding its fascination, the idea of a seizure of power like the assault on the Winter Palace was archaic, and we couldn't say what form the transfer of power to the oppressed classes would take. But certainly a hard shove would be required, it couldn't be a painless transition. No one perceived the connection between socialism (or profound political and social innovation, however one might define it) and democracy as indispensable. It was not present in the political line, and it was not present in the states of mind either, other than as the will of each person to count for something and to speak out.

The apportionment of political space to the left of the PCI was such that in order to exist it was necessary in any case to assume a group form. But we prided ourselves on being an "antigroup group," which worked toward its own dissolution as an organizational form, and included this feature in its political line.

From the very beginning the line we took such pride in had been characterized by two main ideas: work in the union and with the union rather than against it; form worker bodies that did not belong to any group but did not get hidden in the movement either. We called them political collectives; these collectives were to be the brains of the revolutionary process, headed by the working class. Subsequently the idea was extended to youths and to women. In the winter of 1971–72 we had worked to form some CLD's, Women's Liberation Collectives, which helped, as we said at the time, to shatter my contradictions.

My personal condition was like being frozen. Participating in the leadership encouraged an image of "exceptional woman," which blocked the path to an awareness of the condition of women; my personal history removed me from aspects referred to as feminine. I had privileged relationships with the men and too little time to take stock of myself. With the women either I shared the frenzied commitment to politics or else I had almost no relations. In the CLD, created on the impetus of our group, a sort of consciousness-raising had begun, partial, mixed with discussions of problems of a general nature. I was aware of an uneasiness, a being out of place, out of proportion, in that environment. A "masculine" identity hovered about me, in the sense of not accepting the legacy of the mother and of many other women. The denial was in part knowing, it was irritation at the state to which women had been reduced for many centuries. But it didn't know to what extent it was a renunciation of its own potential.

I was frozen in terms of love relationships as well. Almost ossified by now, the affair continued with my first love, the man I had been with for so many years, including a part of the African period. Once more we shared a political and ideal commitment that we put above everything else, and we allowed our relationship to deteriorate into mutual rancor. Sometimes I saw the third friend again—and it was like a breath of fresh air—but he was in another group, with a growing tendency to detach itself from all groups.

APRIL

Everything reappears several times. There was the umpteenth tantrum on account of X, evoked by the sense of exclusion that his new dog causes

me: I can't see it as I would like to, this puppy, sometimes on the phone I
hear it barking or yelping.
For sure I am no longer the free and haughty girl, the father's daughter
who doesn't want to belong to anyone. Lady Pope of the tarot cards,
Sofia. I've passed to the other extreme.
G.: "But now is there somewhere in you the image of the bride?"
"Yes," I answer without hesitating.
"Also the bride of yourself?"
Nice shot, G. is more of a feminist than I am.

Once I experienced the need to be against every authority as a continual
challenge. Now I have begun to accept a relationship of derivation, of
paternity, from some, with their imperfections: one of my professors; my
current superior. I renounce rebellion at all costs.

I ask to see G. more often, to intensify our conversations. We add an hour
on Saturdays. I need a channel for all the excess energy that is currently
diverted toward X.

MAY

Stroll along the Po with the eighteen-year-old children of Zaira, the two
Andreas (one hers, one adopted). They maintain that at least my generation could oppose something and make some choices, they have been
granted much less. They make me tell stories from the seventies, they explain the punk movement to me, their travels, a certain idea of writing
and reading. Listening to them it seems to me that I have not lived in vain.

The same feeling with my women students. The first people who studied
with me and graduated are women. A relationship of friendship has developed with some. I see what they have learned and how they have gone
beyond that, each one in a different way. I discern their ambitiousness
and it frightens me a bit: have I given them that? However, it is right that
they should thrust themselves into the world, that they should obtain
recognition, jobs. Between us there are currents of mutual approbation,
for how we dress, how we talk, not without a constant gentle scrutiny. I
experience what it means to see them go far away, detach themselves:
Perla, who already has one child and is expecting another, but stubbornly
reconciles it all with her work and even continues her research, triumphant, very strong; Sonia, who rejects a permanent job and pursues an ideal

of the single woman, *puella* through and through, embellished with slightly extravagant clothes to remind her of her differentness.

The deadlines of work: classes, theses, meetings. I am like a cadaver in most of these circumstances—*perinde ac cadaver*—except during classes.

Seeing G. an additional time lends sense to the week-end.
The monetary costs no longer worry me. It's true that I have a salary, but it is greatly diminished by my current expenses. Furthermore, G. has raised his rates. I pointed out to him the problems this might create. He acknowledged that it could be a problem, but reminded me that he had warned me of possible increases at the outset. He is very secure, very tough on these matters. I, on the other hand, have always been rather weak about money, at least up to now. I realize that I am beginning to pay more attention to what I spend and how.

JUNE

Cosenza-Stockholm-Minneapolis, once again a period of trips for meetings, a bit neglected because of analysis. G. encouraged me, he doesn't make me pay for the sessions skipped.
I see my friends from New York again, they pick up conversations suspended for years: common work, similar goals, great affectionateness.
I meet other women who are attempting autobiographical writings. For several days I don't feel isolated and strange, but with kindred sisters and brothers who are working in convergent directions. However it's a struggle for me to travel, to be away from G. and from X.

G. says, after having heard some dreams about X:
"Coming to get you from the waiting room, I had the perception that the premature loss of your mother has really left its mark on you."
Well then, my state of orphanhood is so visible. Throughout the day I continue to do the normal things in my job and my routine. In bed, alone, at night, all of a sudden it is as if past time were wiped out, more than forty years. A growing hiccup, an almost asthmatic breathlessness, an absence that takes my breath away: why did you go away, why aren't you here, why did this happen to me? Rancor, hate, terror, I won't be able to survive. Instead, I do survive, groping, like a stump, a wounded part. Scenes come back as vivid as if they were yesterday; the withered

roots become painful. A night spent reliving images of rejection and abandonment.

G. feels responsible.
"One could have not done it."
"That's true, and yet one had to do it."
"Once I wouldn't have done it."
"I realize that it involves a certain risk."
"Risk, yes."
(One technique is to nod in agreement. Another is to repeat the last word, be an echo. X gets nervous, says that I too do it with him more and more often.)
G. emphasizes that he has not acted within a therapeutic strategy. I know that it is very important to him not to hold himself out as healer, doctor, shaman.
But, I explain to him, for me it's crucial, for various reasons, that he said that sentence to me, that he thought that I could deal with it. Because my family, on the other hand, had not thought so and had hidden from me for a long time the fact that she was dead.

Fortunately I see G. more frequently. The condition of neediness has fully reactualized itself: I am stunned, I didn't believe that it really happened in analysis. I had read about it, but always in truculent or sensationalized summaries. Now I am once more the orphan, the stray, the vagabond. I don't have a family, I don't have a refuge, only provisional dens, a tempo-rary roof over my head for the night, precarious houses. For a long time I have feared exhibiting a derelict's face. I resorted to the face of the terri-bly busy person, overloaded with commitments, sure of herself.

Fairy tales from childhood: the one about the little boy who has to have himself chopped up into little pieces and thrown in the lake—but with the magic ring—to slay the dragon.

JULY

I went to hear a prophetess who promises the feminization of our age.
I am enthusiastic about it, I talk about it to G. as if about a discovery. It would provide an answer to my nostalgia for politics and the gospel, life would take on the sense of a mission.
"Life stands on its own two feet," G. objects.

I insist that the teachings of the woman I heard are reconcilable with what I've learned from him.

G. chides me for this retort, he makes fun of me and refuses to agree: "I am not a maestro."

I return home, confused, almost bruised.

I don't know who I was, I don't know what to be. I dream about the two Andreas who don't want coca-cola, but tea, one iced, the other hot. I talk with G. about the two, who have the same name, but are so different.

I report to him the observation of a physicist: we can't give a name to an atomic particle, because it immediately changes positions with another, makes a joke of the principle of identity. It happens to me this way too. I dream about putting on a changing purple dress.

Separation from G. for vacation. One thing I have understood and I owe it to him: better to be alone than to be possessed. On the other hand, I have never wanted to change profession. I prefer to go on being a professor.

AUGUST

Vacation in Sardinia with women friends. During the day we amuse ourselves: we go to the market, we go to the beach, to see the full moon, we cook fresh fish brought by an ex-carabiniere who repeats adventures from the fifties. In the evening we tell fairy tales to the four little girls who are with us, two sets of twins. The image of twins torments me, their being the same and different.

Zaira and I tell each other countless stories about ourselves and people we know. After her initial good opinion, she is a bit polemical regarding X: "He's okay for a while, but he probably isn't really the man for you for the long term?" Maybe there will no longer be a man for me for the long term.

Despite the beautiful days, I can't sleep at night, I count the days that separate me from the end of vacation. It requires too much commitment, too much effort.

I dream about the dark entryway of the old house: a pretty plant of red geraniums; a pot of tiny carnations with the buds tight and still closed, very compact, it's not yet clear what color they will be, whether blue, or pink, as if before a birth.

Why is it so important to remember even just a fragment of a dream?
Because thus I enter the day feeling that my reality is dual, that I have various strata within me. I, the other, and the void, there are at least three of us.

SEPTEMBER

On my return the phone never rings. I check to see that it is connected. Fantasies about what X is doing. Selected so as to repeat the injury suffered as a child.

At the first session with G. he immediately grasps the persistence of the feeling of orphanhood. It reminds him of a great-aunt of his who at fifty introduced herself as an orphan. It makes me laugh and hits the target. In a few years that could be me. The great-aunt, caricature of myself, operates inside me. Laughter dismantles the nightmare of repetition without changes—the Wheel of the tarot cards.

I can't beat colitis and gastritis. My doctor listens to me, visits me, shakes his head: "As long as you're in analysis, there's nothing to do." I know that Freud says it too, but couldn't he give me some cure? No, he asserts, it's useless, in fact, it would be harmful.

OCTOBER

I spend a weekend with friends in the mountains. The nights are very cold, I feel alone and disturbed. For the first time I invoke my mother. I go to sleep, I dream that my father will not regain consciousness.

Every day I discover new sides of my mother: I remember her slender but strong hips, the solidity of the abdomen that carried me and to which I can entrust myself, I feel that she cared about me, I rediscover the security of being loved. I look at a photo in which we are together—I am very little —and I recognize how we are exulting in each other: she lifts me toward the sky triumphantly and I laugh happily. She has a black silk dress with brightly colored flowers. I look at other photos and I discover how I have never seen them. I see that she and my father were a handsome couple, happy, even if only for a few years. I understand that she was strong and brave to give birth to me in spite of her illness. Now I can share her grief in dying so young and leaving me; I can have pity for her fate, as Fay had when I talked about her: "Poor woman," she had said, "who knows how she must have suffered." Fay had felt sorry for her, not for me, I had been upset. Now instead I am able to cry for her, no longer for myself.

I can also resemble her, revive certain aspects of her, continue her: in her love for music, which she played on the piano, in nice clothes, in strength. I can speak to her inner image which I carry within myself. There is no longer rancor, now I have won back my two loved ones, reconciled with each other and with me. I see them shake hands over the kitchen table in our three-person household. I don't know if this scene, so real for me, ever happened.
Conjunction of opposites, falling in love with oneself.
Toward X too there is less rancor. I know about the connections between orphanhood and unhappy love, from Tristan, so named because his mother had died giving birth to him.

Now I too can be a mother, of myself above all. The mother can be happy and sparkling, not terrifying, grim, judgmental. Dancing and joking, like Mom, my American mother, a young girl in body and spirit despite her age. And thus I can confront the last memories, reunite myself with the present.

By the winter of '72-'73 my political and personal crisis was profound. Every day the pointlessness of our efforts appeared more evident: the coup de grace was the occupation of the Fiat plant, when I had the sensation that we were marching around the factory uselessly, casting sidelong glances at a force that couldn't overflow, that couldn't really transform itself into social power. Sensation of a dual impotence, theirs and ours. The weariness was physical too, overwhelming.
The means of salvation was falling in love with a man much younger than myself, sensitive, optimistic. Thanks to him I managed simultaneously to break off my old love affair and my relationship with my group.
Suddenly finding myself outside a community that had been so confined gave me a sense of freedom and of disorientation. I was not in a good state of health and for the first time I felt the need to take care of myself. The continual smoking—my own and that of many others in the subterranean dens that had been our meeting places—had left me with tachycardia and bronchitis. I stopped smoking abruptly and began a new life. I took refuge in feminism, I changed my habits and style of dressing; it was the period of long skirts, clogs and shawls, of brightly colored clothing

frequently borrowed from third world cultures: Latin American sweaters, embroidered sheepskin jackets from Turkey, beaded vests from India. I devoted myself to studying tarot cards and, to a lesser extent, astrology, which fascinated me less, maybe because the people I knew in the field were dogmatic. They assigned to determinative days specific forecasts that didn't prove accurate but caused me a free-floating anxiety at the approach of fateful periods. The following winter I spent a lot of time building furniture designed by Enzo Mari, hammering incessantly to join strips of wood along lines that Eble defined as Babylonian. By now the house was overflowing with furniture. I was also building wooden light fixtures, stringing beads.

I was reading Castaneda's books, which reflected our state, and I talked a lot about it with some friends: the desire to pass from rationality to irrationality, to negate the western ego overturning the relationship with third world cultures established by colonialism and not sufficiently reformed by politics. The West yielded its arms before the magus, science was conquered by magic. The object observed inverted positions and became subject; the customary hierarchies gave up their place to other logics, previously treated as backward and superseded. The anthropologist immersed himself in the culture studied to such an extent that he become its pupil, accepting hallucinations as reality. We too wanted to work through a similar process. I remember a friend, who was still in the group, an intellectual of international renown; in the evenings, when he came back from meetings, we practiced tarot card readings, comparing our different interpretations. He took Castaneda very seriously; when I quoted to him, in one of our nocturnal discussions, the passage in which the author learns from the magus of the possibility of seeing over his left shoulder his own death, which always follows us, he remarked that he had always known it.

For some time I regularly attended a group that met in Milan around Elvio Fachinelli. Along with others, I thought I needed psychoanalysis; he dissuaded us, insisting that this was how we defined the deficiencies in our lives. In that period I had an extraordinary flowering of dreams, messages that had to wait another ten years to be heard. My life was flowing by again. I followed a young friend of mine to concerts by Emerson Lake and Palmer, by Frank Zappa, in the reading of Tolkien, whom we liked for the extreme counterpoise of good and evil, for the demonic vision of power and for its fable-like tone. All this in reaction to the primacy of politics of the preceding years; nonetheless we were taking it up as we had always taken up everything, throwing ourselves into it body and soul, without sufficient detachment.

In that period we theorized the importance for women of relationships *with younger men belonging to a generation less rigidly conditioned by machismo; they were also more acceptable from a feminist perspective. At the time we didn't accept the term "feminism" because it implied a search for parity and for comparability with men, which didn't interest us. We had been developing, along with other women, a radical type of grouping, whose main tactic was forms of communal living. For me it never meant cohabitation in a commune, but we did a lot together, from dancing to dinners, to vacations, even to more specialized practices: discussion groups, consciousness-raising groups, writing groups. We also formed a body expression group, which, starting off from forms of mime taught to us by a French woman, cleared the way for movement and for the expression of the dynamics among us. Body expression, like the other activities, brought out reciprocal aggressivities, not just a desire for sisterhood. There were deep conflicts, expressed and unexpressed. Notwithstanding how difficult all this was to bear—and the difficulties eventually shattered our groups—it was a process of great vitality. Once again I had the sensation of a captivating research capable of changing the world and ourselves, of an exploration at the limits of the known, of a challenge to the established order, with a militant band that was experimenting with new things. The process included forms of violence: in thought, especially in speech. The meetings, or rather the opportunities for larger gettogethers that they offered—at La Tranche, Varigotti, Pinarella—profoundly shook up the stereotypical ideas about women and the relationships among them: that we were orderly, motherly, undifferentiated and helpful sisters. They taught the opposite of their collective and leveling appearance: that there are women, multiple and different subjects in search of themselves, not the woman, with obligatory stages and models.*

In the meantime the implementation of a decision enlarging the university teaching staff to include those ranked in the preceding years' competitions unexpectedly gave me a permanent position. This would have happened in any event, because I had embarked on the normal procedure of indefinite one-year teaching contracts and qualifying courses, but chance took another road; I became an assistant at the university. Thus I had a push—and the time—to resume the studies I had pursued in hit or miss fashion.
It was the mid-seventies. A period of engulfment, of petrification and hermetic closure began for me. In 1975–76 I withdrew from my commitment to life with women, only participating in one group that was investigating our history. The transition from active participation to historical investigation was sudden, even though it continued the form of feminist practice, since the group began by collecting our own memories before those of others. All my activity, increasingly professional, turned in that direc-

tion—memory—with the discovery of oral history. My political activity was necessarily prolonged: it took me a long time to dissociate myself from union activity, however ineffective it might have been, because it seemed impossible not to commit myself at the workplace. The last splash was a series of attempts at mediation, undertaken in '77, between the union and the youth movement at the university, with a proposal for seminars on topics relevant to the movement. The sterility of those attempts was extreme, we were striving to reconcile the irreconcilable.

The subsequent years were years of great discovery for me on the level of historical work. The idea of combining memory and historiography, respecting both, helping to create a method that wasn't detrimental to either, was a wonderful and absorbing challenge. It involved a tremendous amount of work and by now for all intents and purposes I was not doing anything else. After a series of brief romances I was now securely secluded from too many emotions within the confines of a stable living arrangement, which aimed at mutual protection. The cohabitation with Eble had ended, we had both decided to live with other people.
The terrible years of 1978–79 arrived. I remember how every morning I greeted the news of kidnappings and attacks of left-wing terrorism, and especially the days of the Moro kidnapping. In '79 my father's death submerged me in personal mourning, which combined with the collective political and cultural mourning. My loneliness was heightened: my companion was out of the house a lot because of work; my responsibilities at the university were reduced in terms of schedule and contacts with colleagues; almost all my old friendships had been broken off or interrupted with the break-up of the political and women's groups, leaving remnants of bitterness and things unsaid; I spent my days studying and interviewing old people. I ended up developing a type of agoraphobia: it seemed to me that I couldn't withstand the gaze of large numbers of people and that I couldn't raise my own eyes, given all those things that hadn't been cleared up, such as the derivation of terrorist violence from our intellectual and existential milieu. Like many others, I had always assumed that terrorism couldn't come from anywhere but the right, that it was Fascist by definition. We had reacted accordingly, at first glance, to the news of the death of Gian Giacomo Feltrinelli attempting to plant explosives on the scaffolding at Segrate: provocation, frame-up, conspiracy to defame us. But I was also stunned to hear that many were forgetting everything we had said and thought, making sudden transitions from Marxism to liberalism.

We had always changed our ideas. But the hour had come to acknowledge them, to stay the course, not to forget. The reconstruction of mem-

ory was difficult and tortuous. It required remaining as if in quarantine for
years, mulling things over inside oneself, apparently immobile.
The catastrophe had come and gone, without regeneration.
Now I understand my personal path, not evident at the time, of collecting
the memory of Fascism and of nonpolitical forms of anti-Fascism, in order to get at the memory of the next stage, 1968, and of the nonpolitical
forms of continuing it. Physical degradation and aging were my hall-
marks in those years. In '80 I looked much older than now. My way of
dressing was designed to make me look gray, to hide me, to mimic me in
a world deprived of enthusiasms, where I carried on laboriously from day
to day.
A process of purification began with a strict diet and related acupuncture
treatment, suggested by a Steinerian: two years of rigorous attention to
not combining the wrong foods, of those few that were still allowed to
me, reduced to a minimum the opportunities for socializing and sorely
tried those relationships that survived. The diet was part of my long wandering through thoughts and lifestyles, from one sect to another, from one
minority to another, a recapitulation, even if partial, of western and eastern cultures. It was a questioning of order beyond that of the type of
foods, another negation of heritage—of wine, coffee, milk, meat, with all
their symbolic meanings—of the sequence of foods in a meal like the sequence of stages in a fixed history. (In actuality the diet also turned out to
be the means of liberating myself from the stupidest of drugs: I was ad-
dicted to a nasal spray I couldn't breathe without, but which rendered
shorter and shorter the periods between inhalations.)
In order to put an end to the illusions of a final regeneration there needed
to be one last regeneration, which resolutely refused to be final. And here
my story reconnects with the illness discussed in the first chapter. At the
beginning of the eighties I had understood that the journey of life is circular, not linear. And I had to begin my return.

NOVEMBER AND DECEMBER

I dream about the entryway with the mailboxes in the old house: works
done in wrought-iron, works in progress; I go back and forth from the
entryway to the florist, who carries big branches of lilac, and in doing so I
recover a wallet full of money.

X had been promising for months to give me some perfume, but he kept
forgetting. I bought it for myself: it's new, it's called "Insolent," which I
want to translate as insolito, un-usual. G. approved unconditionally.

Need for empty time, pleasure of evenings at home doing nothing specific and listening to music.

There comes to my mind a word used by Guido Viale in talking about
'68: "a contentedness," and I understand that there are some connections
between this, my current, fleeting contentedness, and his of that time, and
that I would like to write something in which I might be able to achieve
something similar, the possibility of entering into life.

X is curious to know who I see, what I do in my free time. Every once in a
while I tell him and finally he blurts out, suspicious:
"But is it possible that you see mostly women?"
It's true. I see them more and more, as friends and as acquaintances, not
for ideology. Through them I glimpse possibilities for myself.
In some I glimpse the dignity of aging. Especially Ester, always elegant,
adorned with rouge and jewels, inclined to see the positive in things and
people, serene even in talking about the eventuality that death may inter-
rupt her research: "In that case—she advises—the materials for the history
of the Montagnana are under the television." At dinner with her and
Sonia, three generations of women. I represent middle age, which acquires meaning with these companions.
One thing that the culture and politics of the vanguard had accustomed
me to was being the first to detect indications, risking a diagnosis even
when things weren't yet ripe. We always did this in time to readjust our
aim. Instead, frequenting the psyche advises always waiting yet another
minute, or in any event is conducive to caution. Everything appears a
second and a third time—maybe many more—even if in changed form.
Nothing proceeds without steps backward, collapses, concessions to its
opposite.

Christmas in Andalucia, with Fay and her friend.
Sunsets and dawns on the sea, the Atlas mountains on the backdrop of the
strait passed by Ulysses.
So Christmas can be not terrible, not obsessed with gifts to get and give,
with family ghosts. There are other bonds of affection and of affinity, capable of distances as of closenesses.
Fay arranged for me to find white roses, red geraniums, and a purple
flower in my room. What madness, to expect that another should realize
your own desires. But it happened, without asking. We take long, long
walks in the mountains covered with thyme and rosemary. Fay talks to
me about her book, which she has been writing for years, on subjectivity,
divided in four sections. It is essential that she write it, for me as well, as a
sign of a way of thinking and of living. Maybe very imperfect, but ours.

We need to acknowledge each other in turn, to present to each other mirrors in which to see reflected our similarities/differences.

Only now is the complementary nature of my two undertakings evident. If I had not heard the life stories of the generation of '68, I would not have been able to write about myself; those stories have nourished mine, giving it the strength to get to its feet and to speak. But I couldn't have borne them, in their alternation of being too full and too empty, if I had not confronted myself and my history with the double motion of analysis and of the exercise of remembering. Now I must make one last shift, the most difficult, regarding the memory of outcomes in the seventies.

Paths of Individuation

6

Diaspora

On the cultural level 1968 acts as a prism: the rays converge on it and emerge from it refracted into different colors. What was invisible previously becomes visible now and at the same time nothing is as it was before. The contradictions have changed their meanings, some problems have undergone a reversal: the relationship between reform and revolution, between right and left. In some instances the implications will be drawn out over periods of decades; some still have not been elaborated, such as the implications of the relationship between ideas and their emotional content or their stimulus to action. In the immediate aftermath disintegration remains the most evident phenomenon: what was united is divided, separated, reduced to dust; individual factors become privileged or frozen; the culture that in the seventies aspires more or less explicitly to '68 is necessarily pluralistic. Not only do the major currents of commitment distinguish themselves—politics, profession—but each current assumes diverse configurations in the trajectory of the life of the individual, and every individual participates, according to the phases of his or her journey, in more than one cultural direction.

All that is not only destruction. It is the fan that opens out as a consequence of the urgency of making choices. What happened imposes itself as something that must be rationalized. It is impossible to continue as before. Now it is necessary to develop, in the form of voluntary assent, something that had been—despite the continuities and the preparations—a spontaneous rupture, the insurgency of a subjectivity still lacking subjects. These latter want to become full-fledged subjects. But, as happens when one emphasizes the conscious element of choices exclusively, these choices will often end up doing the devil's work, bringing about the opposite of what they had promised.

In the here and now, memory is aware of the successive reversals: from the rejection of the party or of work to the commitment to build political organizations or to attain a professional competence. The recollection of the seventies is thus laden with uneasiness; even where it speaks of personal successes, there is something it must justify or avoid. Against its backdrop stands the shadow of a defeat, without the clarity of what exactly has been lost and who has won. The question of mistakes, inside and outside of oneself, remains suspended.

For memory, one method of self-defense is to periodize. Thanks to a typical tactic for saving one's identity, many attribute the "good" to an early and uncorrupted movement, and the degeneration to a subsequent period. The first is situated between the end of '67 and various dates in the following year (March, May, autumn), according to the interpretations of the narrating subject, the geographical site, the events experienced. Aside from differences in periodization and in subtlety, the formula is recurrent:

Marianella Sclavi:
for me '68 ended in '68, as soon as it became the official '68.

Recollection often saves '69, a year in which the workers' struggles flourished, a period of creativity and still a period of movement. Creativity in the original sense of '68, of speech, communication, ability to redefine the concrete:

Guido Viale:
what struck me most about the Fiat workers in the first phase of the struggles was the words they used to talk about them. If you describe the assembly line you do it in certain terms, and instead they described it to you in the language of peasants and shepherds, but they were also talking about their birthplaces in industrial language; this mixing was an authentic moment of creation. Processes of development of new languages existed up to '70. But afterward, the language got sclerotic, even my group's, my organization's.

Only the accounts of some women deviate from the periodizing scheme, accounts that deny an exclusively positive moment to '68 and point out the causes of the decline in the beginning itself, as we shall see later on.

Most of the time the scapegoat in periodization is the transition to real politics, as a separate sphere, as established tradition:

Marianella Sclavi:
the only way of doing politics we had at our disposal after '68, on the outside and among ourselves, was an authoritarian way.

But it is the specific political form into which a large part of the movement of '68 crosses that attracts memory's criticisms: the organizations of the New Left, born or reborn from '69–70 on and lasting until '76. It was a matter of groups that were more numerous, closer to popular and proletarian strata, more current in the area of communications than the groups that animated the sixties had ever been. The majority of my interviewees place the responsibility for the defeat of the original aspirations on the shoulders of these groups.

Franco Aprà:
the New Left groups posed the question of the seizure of power and thus abandoned the problems of content. The tragic outcome was a decade of arguments just about forms of struggle and revolutionary results, where the revolution regarded the form of the state according to the most commonplace interpretation of the most academic Marxism, and not the social transformations that were going on in the meantime. 'Sixty-eight had been a utopia of organizing a huge collective effort, in which I personally participated most willingly. Because I was a little disgusted by a way of coping with the world, a way that later imposed itself as predominant and almost necessary—aggressive individualism. After '68 this working hypothesis was destroyed.

The root of all evil, in this recurrent interpretation, is the question of power, from whence descend the differences—of language and organization—among movements and groups: central political power, not power diffused into everyday situations.

Power and Transcendence

In the collective memory of a majority of those interviewed, the most precarious moment—the moment of transition from movement to groups—is pinpointed just at that instant when the group was still immersed in student reality but was already guided by a general political aspiration. Irene Palumbo provides an example:

> I remember in Naples, no matter what happened, the number one enemy of the Sinistra Universitaria (University Left) was American imperialism. I remember at the mass meetings all the analyses used to start out, "After World War II . . ." and half the crowd would leave because some guy was starting to go through the whole history of American imperialism.

Most of the time the memory doesn't recognize, or doesn't want to pause long enough to take into account, a series of turnabouts: from rejection of politics as an occupation to acceptance of a job as functionary; from denial of the role of vanguard to creation of a revolutionary party; from scorn for the heritage of ideas and experiences of the workers' movement to their revival in an unintentionally farcical tone, with a proliferation of organizational structures such as central committees, control commissions, executives, cadres-schools.

Frequently, in a good faith effort to preserve a legacy endangered by others' machinations, a narrator will depict this passage as unconscious. One woman, who participated in founding the Union of Marxist-Leninist Communists in Rome, blames the Trotskyite Falce e Martello (Hammer and Sickle) group from Milan for having pushed the Union away from the concept of a party deriving closely from the movement and hence endowed with straightforward language and a mass line:

> then the process of degeneration was very fast; this idea of creating a movement that wasn't the party disappeared right away.

In the recollections of the subsequent period, once the phase of transition from the movement was over, the "other," by definition, became the bureaucrat, depicted as someone carrying out his shadowy task without hesitation, completely absorbed in the role of professional revolutionary, even in those organizations that made a point of the spontaneity of the masses (but not of the militants):

Paolo Hutter:
At a certain point I was called in by the Secretary of Lotta Continua who had found out I was smoking hashish, and also because I was hanging out some at "Re nudo"—there were some students we were making contact with to start up the student organization of Lotta Con-

tinua, who did this type of thing. I remember I used to go see some
guys at Cormano, on the outskirts of Milan; we'd roll some joints, listen to music; we'd listen to Jimi Hendrix. And he called me in to order
me to stop because it was against the ethics of the organization, it was
dangerous in that phase, etc., etc.

In contrast, the autobiographical narrative reappraises positively
—even in its expressive vitality—everything about the life of these
groups that didn't pertain directly to the seizure of power: social relationships, study, travel, all the aspects that reflected attitudes and
customs of the movement. Helder Fontanesi concerning his life in
the Union of Marxist-Leninist Communists of Bologna:

I was a little cadre in the process of being formed. And I remember we
studied like mad—but it was a moment that I don't regret for an instant—we were learning about capital, surplus value, Lenin, the party,
the critique of Togliatti. I see the benefit of those years in my work
with the working class, which allowed me to get to know the workers,
including their faults.

If the groups created the possibility of encounters between people
from different social classes and from different places, the memory is
silent regarding the content of those encounters; documentary evidence of them does exist in any case. Rather, the recollection conserves the elements of adventure, of human contact, of connected-
ness with preceding events.

After participating in the student movement at the Milan state university, Romano Madera had helped modify the approach of his
group, the Marxist-Leninist Communist Party of Italy, in a direction
that would be less dogmatic, more open to social movements—a
"Red Line" in contemporary parlance. As part of the effort to rejuve-
nate the Party, Madera, at the behest of the Political Office, made a
trip to the south to check on the strength of the organization. Past
Rome and Apulia, he approached his native soil of Calabria:

I got there after a night on the train, at five-thirty in the morning, and I
got off below Cutro. It's at least five or six kilometers into town and the
road climbs. As I get there there's this huge procession—it's 1969—
there's a black line of men coming down the hill, just like you see in
the neorealist films about the south; some had a mule or donkey, some
had a second donkey carrying their stuff, others coming down with
just one donkey; and then there were those who didn't even have a

donkey, men and women going to work in the countryside. It struck me so much not because it was anything new—I'd seen it as a child—but because in '69, at first glance, it was just the same; this made me roll my eyes and go, "Good God, not a fucking thing has changed here." I go on up, on foot, and find the hero, who I have to say is a really nice guy, with his vineyard and his little house, tiny, poor; nice but eccentric. Extremely good at speechifying, but once you get to the heart of the matter, "Yes, but where's the Party? The Youth Union? I'm from the Political Office (ha ha), I want to hold a meeting," all this spoken with great courtesy because this guy was a legend, nothing. Then, after many hours, getting more familiar, he told it like it was: "I call them and they come." This is the party. He was truly a people's leader, but just that, only a people's leader. Absolutely impossible to establish any program, have a meeting, because he couldn't answer any sort of question about the structure of the organization. And it wasn't because he was pretending. The problem was just that in reality the Party didn't exist.

The memory of political journeys assumes an important role in the biographies; geographical relocation reinforces social and ideal mobility. After her experience in Gioventù Studentesca (Student Youth), the Milanese movement of '68, and involvement at the Autobianchi factory as part of Lotta Continua, Franca Fossati was sent by Lotta Continua to Frankfurt. She stayed there two years, agitating primarily at the Opel factory:

We tried to organize among the foreign workers, on a multinational level, with respect to all the nationalities of the immigrants there in other words. At that time there was still Fascism in Greece, there were Greek exiles, there were Turks, there were Spaniards who'd had experience with workers' committees (*comisiones obreras*). The Greeks and Turks had a really rigid Marxist-Leninist approach to their politics; we were into spontaneity, but we were much more dogmatic than the Germans, with our sociological framework involving class analysis; the Germans were already swept up in feminism and devoted a lot of time to taking care of their private lives. Anyway, to homogenize all these languages was a thankless task, plus the fact that we didn't even know German! For example, there was the slogan "Strike in October," and I remember leaflets that began "*Streik in Oktober,*" in Turkish "*Ekinda grève,*" "*Huelga in octubre,*" "*Sciopero in ottobre*"; and, more or less following the same text the various groups would write the flyer in all these languages and those who could understand each other would agree on it. Turkish, Greek, Slavic, Spanish, Italian, German: I think these were the languages that we could count on producing. The translations were really complicated, and some we even had to do by hand since none of the typewriters had Greek characters.

Alternating with these lively tones are the somber tones of mistakes made, the evocation of feelings of defeat long shunted aside by collective pride, the emptiness after comrades have scattered. Those who continue to be politically active today have deduced the implications of this conglomeration of acceptances and renunciations in their autobiographical narratives, and they have, as a result, reshaped the orientation and sense of their politics.

Franco Russo, leader of the Trotskyite FGCI in the sixties, then of the Roman student movement, of the Nuclei Comunisti Rivoluzionari (Communist Revolutionary Nuclei), of Avanguardia Operaia (Workers' Vanguard), now deputy from Democrazia Proletaria (Proletarian Democracy):

> I believe that the revolution does have its potential, but in the sense
> that Kant said: "It's a normative idea." Fortunately, we probably won't
> seize power—this is a major shift for me with respect to the past. I believe that today the basic issue is the ongoing critique of power. This is
> really what the seventies gave us.

Piero Bernocchi, who has followed the same political course as Russo since 1968, takes a different approach to political continuity—he works for a free radio station, and he has deliberately rejected two elements from his past, an emphasis on long-range projects and a charismatic role:

> Over the years I have re-examined and modified my ideas. Today, I am
> more interested in transforming what's there, making the city and the
> country healthier in every sense, increasing equality, justice, cleaning
> things up physically, fighting pollution, improving the quality of life
> in the city, getting rid of traffic and freeing people, letting them get
> around more easily. All these things were once considered irrelevant,
> insignificant, and now they're important. You ought to live your projects here and now. It's a tougher road, and it's less gratifying than the
> old way of fantasizing distant goals without specifying what the stages
> would be, and how they would actually come about.
>
> On a personal level, it happens a lot that I talk to people who don't

know that I've written three books, hundreds of articles, tons of leaflets, at least partially led a movement, that I've been politically active for sixteen years, they don't know and I've never told them; it doesn't matter to me. But at first it was an effort, because I got a lot of gratification out of this world of the New Left that still exists; they give you back the glory of the past, and it's ego-gratifying. So it's an effort and every once in a while it's tempting. You'd like to say, "But you don't know who I was." I'd rather say: "Try to see who I am now," even if I'm probably not a big deal, rather than fling all the junk from the past at them.

The picture presented up to now is one side of the coin of memory, perhaps the most valid, one I shared when I began my pilgrimage from one interviewee to another. After attempting an inventory of this collective memory, I feel that it is precisely the demise of the question of power that is the central grief hanging over the entire seventies and casting its long shadow on us still. To be sure, critiques of the groups could and should be even more purposeful than those reported. However, in a rough, anachronistic, and authoritarian fashion, those New Left groups posed the question of something that extends beyond the quotidian. They emphasized it to the exclusion of other issues, but evading that question leaves a void that can be denied only at a still undetermined cost.

It seems to me today that posing the question of power was a way of recognizing transcendence, in the secular sense, as the act of transcending toward meaning by an intercommunicating subject, to quote a master, Ernesto De Martino; as a shared project of moving beyond all possible data, of forcing the march of history by means of a participation capable of interpreting it and restoring objectivity to it thanks to an affirmation of extreme subjectivity. In contrast with the also-current theses of the complete immanence of the political in the quotidian, the groups posed the ultimate question, even as they were formulating it—in the case of the most astute—as a prospect totally different from the seizure of the Winter Palace. The vocabulary and the organizational forms used belonged to the past; the prospects for the future were unfairly cut short. But this attitude sustained an ethical tension and a constant effort to participate in reality and to understand it. Even the acceptance of internal hierarchies had a positive side: direct democracy had been forced to come to terms with the delegation of decision-making power; agreeing to defer one's own interest without giving up control, to place one's trust in others, to make differences among individuals public rather than keeping them hidden, all this could lead to a greater maturity.

I fear that the repression of the issue of power may result in a revival of the excessively rosy attributes of a culture believed to be without blemishes or weaknesses, dedicated to victory over the villains of history, superficially optimistic. It is true that the by-products of that culture have ended up emphasizing its negative aspects: the concept of individual rights has been subsumed into extreme forms of corporatism; concern for the individual's own situation has been surpassed by a victimism that looks elsewhere for the solution to his or her own problems, or by a twisted conspiracy theory that holds enemy plots accountable for the failings of individual undertakings. But even the hearty optimism of those who have taken account of the need for micropolitics risks a reduction, albeit of a nature opposite to that of the seventies.

Let us pause here for a moment to ascertain our path. Our purpose is not a historical reconstruction but rather a mulling over and internalizing of some memories that remain too external to ourselves, too objective. The experience of the groups was in fact completely objectivized, too lacking in subjectivity for the needs of the times, capable of transcendence only in a totally external sense. It is not surprising that the result has been a loss of that presumed objectivity as well. Perhaps it is necessary to shift direction in order to re-evaluate that experience or salvage something from it. One cannot fail to raise the problem of the relationship with power, even in its grandest and remotest forms. At the same time one cannot deny that processes for the dispersion of power came into being. One possibility is to frame the issue as the relationship between one self and another, as a comparison with the uncontrollable, the unchangeable, and even, in certain respects, with evil. Taking this direction into account, one remains free to address the opposite side of the problem, which must necessarily be posited as the link between power and democracy at the highest levels. Lacking that, the groups' experience in the seventies winds up being either contemptible or ridiculous. For this reason—and as prefiguration of the future—I consider it indispensable to keep in mind the other side of the coin, that side exhibiting the aching mark of loss, the search for error, the acknowledgment of mourning. There are some whose memories of the end of that period are of a dramatic upheaval that cannot be attenuated with false consolations.

Luigi Bobbio:
That period is unrecognizable, it's devoid of meaning. I too got a lot out of my political experience, but not much of it is usable. The changes one goes through in that type of experience are almost com-

pletely useless. According to me, there is still a void, an absence that is difficult to fill, because, even if that presence was dark, it leaves an absence that's more dramatic. There are roads to individual happiness, everybody has one or another, even I probably have one, but I don't find them all that convincing, when it comes right down to it. It seems to me there is a hidden bitterness that actually has a hard time coming out, because there's also a defensiveness about these things. You don't talk about them or you talk about them on an anecdotal level. Like saying, "I don't recognize myself any more."

Others recall the origins of what could be called a culture of resentment, which became the context for recourse to violence as a routine matter, without a balancing of objectives, or for a retreat into solitude, into "the tide of privacy."

Romano Madera:
I have always made a humongous effort to understand others, to tolerate different positions, oh well! to consider the average level of the masses and to be sensitive with respect to other groups too. All this turns around psychologically into, "I no longer give a shit."
We were losing ground in the general disinterest, in '74 the New Left groups were already undergoing a 180-degree conversion—and that's when a terrible disgust came over me, because I couldn't stomach seeing people, who up until six months earlier had said just the opposite, now, pushed by increasingly difficult political circumstances, undergoing disastrous conversions to the right, with "long live the trade unions" and "long live the PCI." "Okay, but then it's something even worse than paranoid delirium, then it's not that you wanted a revolution, because if you did you'd act completely different. You've found this identity—like I myself did, but I'm losing it while you're not—as politicians, as political hacks rather, anything goes as long as you can hang on to some function within this universe." That's exactly what happened to so many people, resentment because we hadn't gotten anywhere.

In this climate the movement of '77 was born, combining the rejection of the question of power and the sense of tragedy at its loss with a dual reaction that ran from the macabre to the arcadian.

Marino Sinibaldi:
Renunciation, writing off promises of transformation, this was the climate; when there's a catastrophe, the plague—the stories of the Middle

Ages—a sort of mindless joy, frivolity spreads. 'Seventy-seven in
Rome was this more than anything else; you played games and joked
and hung around together all day, you did recreational drugs in a
totally happy, liberated way, without feeling guilty, you met lots of
people. There were the gardens at the university, it was the warmest
February in history, it was sunny and there were already daisies and
everyone hung out there on the grass, tons of people, all the people
that I used to hang around with—I'm going to have a child now with a
girl I more or less met there. There was an element among us that only
lay around among the daisies, and there was an element that only took
up arms, but there was also an element in between.

Sinibaldi is one of the few whose biography reflects a continuum
between '68 and '77. Notwithstanding the hostility between the protagonists of '68 and those of '77, corroborated in many memories, the
continuity is not only biographical. 'Seventy-seven recapitulated
themes from '67–'68—lifestyle, "each individual proceeds from his
own needs"—but without the transfiguration of politics, because
"at that moment there were no politics" (Maderna). Politics as the
struggle with central power no longer existed; it had faded into the
imagination.

The Fantasy of War

The connections between the movement of '68 and terrorism are one
of the most difficult historical problems of recent decades. In addition to the scarcity of investigations there is a nebulous aversion to
talking about it, a burden of prejudices and bitternesses, a sense of
taboo. The memory of my interviewees only nibbles at the edges of
the question without getting to the point of posing it. Some of these
protagonists have served years in prison on charges of insurrection,
membership in an armed band, participation in moral support of terrorist activities. The judicial proceedings concerning them have
sometimes resulted in acquittals; in other cases the proceedings are
still suspended, or await further steps. To be sure, the group of narra-
tors who appear in this book is too small and chosen on the basis of
other criteria—importance in '68, relevance on the level of subjectivity—to allow drawing any conclusions about continuity and discontinuity between terrorism and '68. I should not like to evade the
problem, however; I will make use of other data to express some observations on this matter, in a still purely hypothetical fashion.

Certainly one cannot sustain the hypothesis of a massive crossover of militants from the environment of the student movement of '68 to the armed struggle in a terrorist sense. The direct derivations in theoretical terms are also rather slim, especially because of terrorism's poverty on this score. Still, continuities exist, in the tortuous derivation that characterizes the biographical journeys and the evolution of ideas. These appear when one considers the so-called second generation of left-wing terrorism, composed of people born between 1950 and 1960.

Several collections have come out of the memories of this in-between generation, which represented the majority of the personnel implicated in acts of political violence in the seventies and early eighties. Those memories contain contradictions, slips, and lacunae of great interest, and of difficult interpretation. With respect to '68, they treat it in general as an antecedent with imprecise contours. The recollection of '68 is vague and reduced, overshadowed by more important events—for the narrating subject—which took place subsequently. On the level of biographical structure there is little relevance either; the student movement occurs during the high school years, a fact that is not determinative per se, but that in these specific biographies assigns a secondary role to it.

A few examples, coming from research in progress. Nadia Mantovani, born in 1950, member of the strategic leadership of the Red Brigades, held in the Bologna jail:

No, '68 was not a turning point for me. I was attending high school in a town in the province of Mantua, we had a lot of social activities with classmates, and the movement activity was totally absorbed by that. It was the years at the University instead—I enrolled in Medicine at Padua—that were determinative and changed my life. I hung out with Toni Negri's group, but the most important thing was the worker agitation at Marghera.

Susanna Ronconi, born in 1950 in Venice, member for a brief period of the Red Brigades and then of Prima Linea (Front Line), in '67–'68 was in her fourth year at the science high school. Regarding the occupation of the Catholic University of Milan, of Palazzo Campana in Turin, she has almost no recollection. For her it is the following academic year, '68–'69, that looms larger in her memory:

I remember wonderful collective moments, the way of being in there with enthusiasm, with curiosity. Seminars, cultural activity, more than anything else. School as territory to conquer and manage in the first person. The discovery of the possibility of living collectively and of living well.

But for this narrator, too, "life will change drastically later on when she chooses the militancy of Potere Operaio," that is, with her enroll-ment in the political science faculty at Padua in the academic year 1969–70, and her attendance at Negri's classes, "essentially cadres-schools," "the only truly formative moment" in an entire political ca-reer. In this biography other external circumstances come forcefully into play:

> as I began to live inside the movement, one of the first things I came to grips with was the problem of the presence of the Fascists, which was very heavy in Padua. The idea of a part of the state on the side of the clandestine Fascist right was something I got used to quickly. Being in the collectives that organized demonstrations, the problem of "watch out for the Fascist" was a habit I acquired almost immediately, in a fairly confrontational way too. Then when the massacre at Piazza Fontana happened, it was a very important moment. I remember my first encounters with workers, with ex-partisans: the discussion about the "Resistance betrayed" and about vigilance. There was a definition of left along a range of 180 degrees, in the sense that the assemblies ranged from anarchist to socialist. I felt the push to assume a presence that would be more political and responsible.

The particularity of the Paduan experience should not be inter-preted as absolutely exceptional. The experiences of Silveria Russo, also born in 1950 in Turin, and affiliated with Prima Linea, pass through different political stages: Falce e Martello in '66–'67 when she is in her second year at the classical high school, the student movement of Palazzo Campana the following year, worker agitation at Lingotto and Rivalta for Lotta Continua in her first years at the uni-versity, feminist groups in subsequent years. In '76–'77 Silveria Russo will participate in Prima Linea's armed actions; for these she is serv-ing a sentence that includes two life terms.

As one can guess even from these few examples, the filter of the in-dividual biography transforms and directs the influences received from the family, from the environment, from circumstances. No sin-gle one of the cultural and social conditions is determinative; many have felt the heritage of the Resistance betrayed, the necessity of com-batting neo-Fascism, but not all have done so with arms. The definitive decision is up to the subject, even if we know how complicated and stratified subjectivities and the relationship between individual and collective may be. But final responsibility given to the individual is the only way of safeguarding the full subjectivity of the individual.

The accounts quoted remind us that vast intellectual and political environments shared a discourse on violence that included the urgency of actively defending oneself. Surrounding this was the aura of a fantasy of revolution as armed struggle, populated by mythical figures such as Che Guevara, the fighters in Vietnam and in other liberation struggles, including the Resistance to Nazi-Fascism. This is a link with '68.

A recollection from the movement in Trent:

Marianella Sclavi:
Che Guevara had just been killed and we organized a commemorative
assembly with a flyer entitled: "Che Guevara is Alive," in which we
celebrated armed struggle, putting in Echevarria, Camilo Torres,
against the rich bourgeoisie drinking champagne, against the dictator-
ship that prevents you from protesting, so there's not democracy. . . .

The question remains as to why some did not pay attention to this fundamental clause—"if there's not democracy"—and decided that they were able and obliged to realize a vision, which instead remained just that for many who shared it. But in the mid-seventies a body of opinion already existed to which even nonmilitants of the groups subscribed, which continued to talk with the real terrorists or to consider them "errant comrades." The slogan "neither with the State nor with the Red Brigades" was born in that atmosphere, which, rather than renounce the identities of the past, nourished a vision by now complicit in crimes.

We have gone a long way from '68 and from its most authentic spirit. What was in between? Once again memory, even of the youngest, answers: a reaction to the mentality of the groups, to their pan-politicism, to the ideologization of the legacy of the student movement. C.R., born in Rome in 1954, member of "Viva il Comunismo" (Long Live Communism) during high school, then moved to Turin and from '76 participant in the area of Autonomia (Autonomy), member of the minor terrorist organization Nuclei Comunisti Territoriali (Territorial Communist Nuclei), served two years in jail for participation in an armed gang and theft. In 1968 he was in his first year of science high school in Rome:

I experienced '68 in the stories of older brothers, because basically

it was a university students' event. With '69 we too came on the
scene.

There were these meetings, these assemblies with older kids, who
maybe wore Mao Tse-Tung buttons. The first times they held these
assemblies at the Camera del Lavoro, at the University, there was a
total difference in language. I remember, when I went to the assemblies, these university students started off—I remember they were all
really thin, with big beards and really long hair, it seemed like they
didn't eat for days and days and every once in a while their voices
would give out, evidently the tenth assembly of the day. And they
talked about revisionism, about social-imperialism, we couldn't even
really comprehend what they were talking about.

The responsibilities of the groups in the tortuous paths that lead to
the privileging of violence lie, at the least, in the transmission of a
mentality—or frequently in the reactions induced by such a mentality—and in the development of confused political personnel such as
elements of the *servizi d'ordine*; already accustomed to mindless violence, these latter were easy prey for terrorist ideologies. But one cannot forget that it is primarily with the disappearance of the New Left
groups that the violence, both terroristic and scattered, intensifies, a
violence that most of the time no longer aspires to guerilla warfare
waged to seize power; in accord with Hannah Arendt's insight, with
the disappearance of politics, violence exercised as an end in itself,
no longer as a means accepted by force of circumstance, takes precedence. Memory recalls the absence of hope in such a situation.

Helder Fontanesi, born in Reggio Emilia in 1948, came from a family of peasants and workers, half Communists half Catholics—father
a partisan, uncles and mother couriers in the Resistance; a model
student in high school, he enrolled in medicine at Bologna in '67,
participated in the student movement, in a factory agitation over
dangerous working conditions, then belonged to the Unione dei
Marxisti-Leninisti (Union of Marxist-Leninists). In '74 he decides to
move to Turin, where he manages to get hired at the Fiat Mirafiori
plant. In '75 he abandons his organization, chooses as his new reference point Rosso, (Red) because "it is far and away the most separate," and creates an autonomous collective at Mirafiori:

Autonomia encompasses the worker tendency that is coming apart,
encompasses the disintegration of Lotta Continua, encompasses the
fringes of anarchism, encompasses the Marxist-Leninists who couldn't
stand it any more, and encompasses social behaviors: expropriation,
going to the movies and not paying, that were there as givens, even

before Toni Negri gave them a political license. There were the workers' marches at Fiat, equipment thrown around the factory floor, broken plate glass windows, fleeing scabs, section bosses beaten up. When Autonomia's thematics intervene, one seeks to induce this violence directly, see? The proletariat expresses violence? I theorize proletarian violence as the moment of communication-conflict with the society. Terrorism is something else, it has different values, it has a different theoretical formulation, there's the Party, there's the assault on the Winter Palace. . . . Gradually as the political spaces are narrowed—the State presses, terrorism presses—Autonomia is crushed. Then one part of us says, "Fine, it's over," and then you enter into private life of necessity, because you aren't willing to go into the PSI, the PCI, Manifesto, DP, but not into Prima Linea or the Red Brigades either. After '79 terrorism becomes the sole owner of the terrain.

With respect to the explosion of subjectivity that had been '68, the period of terrorism represents a drying up and a diversion of the subjective force, which no longer succeeds in conferring objectivity on the world and in intervening to change it.

Professionalism and Modernization

Let us return to '68. Starting out from 1968, a series of paths has been tried and exhausted, sometimes straying too far from the original inspiration. This necessitates a process of back-and-forth that resumes from the point of departure and follows another series of directions, mental and practical.

According to Franco Aprà, architect,

a consequence of '68 is even now alive inside some heads, mine for example: thinking that what counts is the result of your work, more than any personal recognition; conceiving of a socially useful work. That's it, this way of thinking, I still have it, even today I have a relationship with '68, which is to introduce elements of quality into my work and to consider as positive every doubt that leads to deciding with a maximum of awareness.

Anna Trautteur preferred teaching to working in her father's firm:

I don't know to what extent it's the fruit of '68 or a quirk of mine that made me participate in '68—I was always among the anonymous figures of the movement—I can't live the events of my life in a passive manner. In my school I immediately became responsible for a school-family committee, I was the one who pushed certain experiments for a program of modernization, which I've now been doing since '77. I've always done all this without being linked either to a political party or to a well-defined group or to a union. A political career doesn't interest me, what interests me is working inside institutions to try to improve them.

Similar consequences of '68 find as many variations on the theme as there are forms of innovative commitment. The continuities are highlighted particularly in the form of professional competencies, where new jobs have literally been invented.

Luciano Del Sette, journalist and writer, mainly of texts on travel in places still not easily accessible by mass tourism:

From '68 I absorbed the will to make choices. My mode of traveling is also the fruit of what it had meant to speak out, to meet others, to demonstrate, to hear that certain ideas had a following. That is, I can't keep still, and in my opinion this is a great lesson that '68 taught you; if you want to grow old well, if you want to achieve your own maturity, you always and only do it by looking for new terrains to discover.

But the derivations are not direct. Peppino Ortoleva, free-lance historian of the media, observes that many of those who held positions of importance in the student movement are active today in the field of mass communications, and he singles out another joke of history, a reversal from intentions to practice:

if to be a leader, for example, of the PCI, you could learn to write, but also [learn] managerial and organizational skills and concepts, in '68 we learned primarily to speak, to write, to get others to talk, to launch slogans. . . . Now we all live, to some extent, on the earnings from what we learned then.

In '68, one of the biggest targets of our critique was in fact the system of the media. TV, with its fake objectivity, with its ability to make all its spectators passive, with its conformism, could be a good symbol of what wasn't right. We opposed to it our communication, which we wanted to be egalitarian, active, rebellious. Maybe, unwittingly, all we did was to anticipate the new landscape of communications, differentiated (a VCR in every house) and interactive (the personal computer), even if certainly not egalitarian. The world of the media today is in part the nightmare of our dreams, but the skills we developed then fit in well there.

Contrary interpretations of all this are possible. One that emerges clearly and finds validation in the historiography of the period is an analysis of '68 as the moment of modernization with respect to an archaic society. Pedro Humbert, director of a large telecommunications company:

You were a participant in a movement of democracy, of antiauthoritarianism. These were the values that fraternized—I want to use this slightly nineteenth-century term—all the students. Within the blanket of ideology one often wanted to define as revolutionary that which had a whiff of democratization, an element of progress, of cultural warfare, against an immobile society where the distance between classes hindered socializing. Those elements have been denigrated by a connotation of "revolutionary" that denied the element of modernization. But if you look today, beyond the political party chosen, at the professional occupation of many who were cadres either at my level or at a higher level, you will find methods of taking the initiative in a new manner, for example in the method of merchandizing certain products, in strategies for innovative marketing, or else in the choice to work on advanced, modern trends.

For some the continuity of experience is not merely professional but political, an element of "struggles defined in a strong reformist sense," as in Naples, where "democratic advances, even minimal, must all be achieved with long battles (Franco Barbagallo, professor of history). For others the political signal has changed, with an umpteenth reversal. Renato Musto, professor of theoretical physics:

We contributed in our deeds, involuntarily, to creating a society in large measure different from the preceding one. We created, for better or worse, a democratic attitude in many places. However, what we tried to graft onto this, the critique of the social systems, has been erased. The most striking thing is that the memory has been erased, that is, transformations took place, new characters were created who have new customs and new ways of behavior that are the average habits of advanced countries. But the attitude of critique, which was the soul of '68, has gotten lost. And what was supposed to go with the

democratic attitude—that there must be a certain sense of consciousness in every subject—this has disappeared. There is a continuity that
is born from our defeat, not from our victory.

The fact that some part of those political skills has flowed into the
unions and the parties, in a process that is still taking place, is in-
escapable. The judgments, always closely tied to the particular personal experience, are contradictory.

Guido Viale:
In the years '77–'79, anyone who thought his role was that of permanent militant and thus did not decide to quit when the movement
ended faced two outcomes: either terrorism, or the union and the left-
wing parties. This made me reflect, saying: "I don't want to take either
of these two roads, so the only way of fighting these outcomes is not to
do anything political anymore."

Today Viale is engaged in social research, primarily commis-
sioned by public agencies:

I am good at certain things on account of my experience: for me, doing
a couple of interviews and reconstructing a working organization or a
social situation is very easy, on the basis of my ability to make use of
the direct relationship, to understand how a situation stands, acquired
through long years of political experience. The culture of '68, broken
down into its tiniest forms, became the material, the bricks for establishing the social knowledge indispensable to the managerial culture.
But I don't think that my personal fulfillment is in my profession. I understand that some may seek it there—maybe at one time I would have
accused them of collaborationism—but it's not the case for me. In a
profession I'm looking for money and free time and, to put it bluntly,
little effort.

Beyond the divergent political evaluations it is undeniable that
there was a modernization and that '68 contributed to it. Despite the
enthusiasms of individuals, the limits and the imperfections of the
related process of democratization are such as to leave many doubts
about its historical value. From the point of view of individual destinies and their assumption of meaning, which is what matters to us
here, that which had been joined together has once again been sun-
dered and the gap seems unbridgeable.

Marco Revelli:
the modernizing character was one of the nuclei of identity of '68. A youth culture capable of speaking to a nonyouthful universe, of entering into a relationship with the entire social universe, of taking a position on the struggles of the Michelin workers, on international politics, on the curriculum, on school, to be able to argue with anyone. This had attracted a lot of people, but for them modernization was enough, while we wanted to define innovation and the break with normality in a leftist sense. Afterward our paths diverged once again. . . .

One meaning of that divergence is that '68 by now belongs to everyone, it does not have favored heirs. And at times it exists more in its denial than in its literal continuation.

Women Keep Their Distance

The derivations from '68 delineated so far establish a complex and contradictory field, which also includes drastic contrapositions. Nonetheless, the diverse positions—which may speak from integration or through destruction/subversion—are fighting over the same patrimony. Patrimony, in fact, heritage of the father. On the other hand, there is a position, as we mentioned at the beginning of this chapter, that repels it, sometimes totally, sometimes simply keeping its distance. It is the position of some witnesses, not all of whom are connected with the women's movement.

We have already seen that in recent decades the processes of female emancipation have included interweavings of affirmation and of inferiority. The search for parity has often ended up turning into competition and imitation, rather than becoming the basis of its own subjectivity. For many women, reflection on all this has sharpened the sensitivity to something already felt in '68, but not expressed then for lack of words.

For Paola Di Cori (1946), who had moved, with some trauma, from the cosmopolitan environment of Buenos Aires (where her parents had taken refuge to escape the racial laws) to a conservative Roman high school, '68 at the philosophy faculty had been a moment of learning and of exciting commitment; but recollection restores the perception of some discomfort:

> I considered myself absolutely at the lowest level, because I am a very slow person, and in discussions it takes me a long time to understand

what's going on or to take part, I get lost—I kept trying to understand where I was living. . . .

Her discomfort is heightened by the transition to a phase in which "no one studied any more," and above all by the "imposition of an absolutely unreal model of free sexuality":

> just the idea that you had to have these sexual relationships casually, which you talked about—both men and women—in their technical aspects: "He's impotent, he can't do it," chilled me.

Memory also introduces a discourse of exclusion and extraneousness for those women who appeared to be at the center of the movement and of its leadership. Fiorella Farinelli, who had participated in all the struggles of the sixties at the Normal School in Pisa, says of herself:

> I was always a little bit backward, I didn't understand things well. . . .
> I was self-repressed and also frustrated at not having individual autonomy. I experienced, as fiancée of one of the leaders and friend of many others, a personal and political relationship in which, however, I was not an equal.

For her, autonomy would come about through the birth of a daughter, the discovery of solidarity with other mothers, and responsibility as a leader of the school union. An itinerary comparable in certain respects to that of Marianella Sclavi, active right from the beginning of the Trent student movement:

> I had never fully accepted being a female. The first time I accepted it, right in my innermost being, was when I gave birth to my daughter, and I was twenty-seven years old.

Her autobiographical account is particularly interesting in laying bare the contradictions of the emancipatory forms preceding the women's movement. As live-in partner of Mauro Rostagno, a fixed role awaited her—as the leader's girlfriend, so much so that at times she refused to make speeches at the assemblies, something she used to do very easily before. But most of all that role separated her from the women who were laboriously searching for their identities, at times along forced paths:

these girls had their drama—"I'm still a virgin, how can that be? I have to find a way to eliminate the problem"—which I looked upon with something of a maternal spirit.

And yet some opened new roads, unthinkable for those who saw them as

young girls a bit sheltered, provincial . . . in other words it was compli-cated for me to have a relationship with them—and instead, while all these things were happening, they grew and changed, they wrote a book like *La coscienza di sfruttata*. Ultimately I discovered for myself that these girls had completed their whole development, and it made me really happy, but I absolutely didn't know how it had happened.

The condition of those who, in many circumstances, had for years found themselves "the only woman" tended to perpetuate a condi-tion of isolation and of contraposition with other women. Eliana Minicozzi, after having participated in '66 in the occupation of the University of Rome over the death of Paolo Rossi (a leftist student who died after a clash with Fascist students in 1966) and in '68 as a university assistant in the movement in Naples, had successfully overcome the trials of male politics, acquiring the stamp of "bravura" within the Sinistra Universitaria ("the praise of the leadership who said, '*Mamma mia,* you're really something'").

That role carried with it costs and loneliness even in regard to the younger women or women at the lower levels, from whom a tradi-tion, a language, a way of feeling separated her:

I believe that some women hated me, because later I re-encountered them in the women's movement and they told me so. Trying to orga-nize the women's collectives—consciousness-raising, etc., etc.—their aggressiveness with respect to me came out. Because I was always part of the leadership. I was the leader, I was the one up there who had to use the same language as the males in order to have gotten to the point of leading.

Their relationship with politics wasn't my relationship with politics. And they didn't understand this even when I explained it, they took it mostly as snobbery. I cried when Stalin died, because in my house you cried, Stalin was the grandpa. These political things for me were blood, see, not brains, it was the family imprinting. In '69 we were at odds with the PCI, so we didn't go to the demonstrations, but when I encountered the bus with the red flags, the workers who were singing

"Bandiera rossa," I cried in my car, because of the impossibility of returning to that world.

The account of one of those younger women records her relief at losing the obligation of "bravura," acknowledges a continuity from the students' movement to the women's movement, affirms the difference.

Irene Palumbo (1951):
there is continuity in the sense that there is the value of solidarity, which I feel as common to the two movements, of antiauthoritarianism, of the sense of democracy. However the big difference lies directly in the man/woman relationship. I felt that at the assemblies the men were much better at speaking, they were much stronger, they were the ones who had the power, and maybe you counted if you were the girlfriend of that important man or in any event if you were good at doing some things. But you always had to put yourself in a competitive or demonstrative relationship: if you didn't know how to speak, but you were able to hand out a hundred fliers in half an hour, you were good for that. And instead with the women, no, you didn't *have* to be good.

In different ways these women allege their partial alienation from a movement that nonetheless frequently represented a political birth for them no less than for their male comrades. But the real birth would take place elsewhere, according to this memory, later. Or perhaps its roots were anterior, as the account of Serena Nozzoli, who was in the movement at the State University of Milan from the outset, suggests. She remembers '68 as a

tormented period in many respects. A tremendous isolation, a moment of great incomprehension and inability to find solidarity. It wasn't a choice on my part. I was just there, going to State in '68.

The narration describes the contrast between a desire for individual probing and the spread of collective examinations; between the constant presence "at assemblies, at demonstrations, at takeovers" and the sense of "a growing distance and suffering." There are tones of negative prophecy, almost Cassandra-like:

I had already seen terrorism in '68. I told my friends so, but they always said I was crazy: . . . the feet on the professor's desk, bringing up

Che Guevara as a monographic topic for the economics exam, with this insolent pretense, this arrogance provided by numbers . . . things slightly reminiscent of Mussolini's thugs that, however, all seemed like revolutionary demonstrations, while I saw in them a type of violence, of nonculture and of passivity, taking advantage of the mob to do things they wouldn't have done by themselves. . . .

This position fits into a firm self-representation that depicts itself as unchanged from infancy to later misfortunes:

> I have always been unwell
> from childhood I've nurtured an intense rebellion against
>   the way in which women were treated, at home
> I am always me.

Women's distancing themselves from '68, partial or total, sends at least two important messages. It is a critique of the left, of its way of thinking and of doing politics, it is a way of identifying itself as outside one tradition in order to establish a new and different tradition. The second message is that the women's movement affirms origins other than those of the student movement, which it doesn't consider its direct antecedent. Here it is necessary to distinguish historical origins, genesis, and representation, including self-representation achieved; it is necessary to interpret the memory about this separation. Pushed too far it arrives at an assertion of women's difference so accentuated as to reject essential heritages—or convergences: unilateralness, speaking out, nullification, critique of ordinariness, relevance of emotional stirrings, and collective commitment. These are just as much values of '68, which, however, was incapable of fully recognizing, as the women began to do, the importance of the differences among individuals. But this last theme itself must be tempered with an affirmation of equality and democracy. To find the right tone it is necessary to set aside the antihistorical attitude shared by the movement of '68 and the women's movement and not blanket with amnesia the patrimony of free thought: to recoup from the fathers all that serves us—with an act of memory that harks back beyond the most recent past.

Lives and Life Histories

The search for what '68 produced in cultural terms can't stop at veri-

fying the proliferation and the abandonment of various thematics.
The process, in its complexity and at the point at which it has arrived
today, has also been preeminently one of shaping lives. In the course
of its stages—the break-up of the previous communities of family and
friends, the establishment of new fusionist communities and the subsequent splitting up of these second communities as well, with periods of isolation and individual crises—individuals are molded who
did not exist before, and who themselves represent the results of a
great cultural shift as well as being its carriers.

Nadia Ghesini:
I'm not able to partition the person who did '68 and who with her individual story goes one place, goes another place, does politics in yet
another. We are also ourselves, basically. Then we made our choices,
fought our battles, did our things.

Taking this observation seriously, we can say that in the first place
the culture of '68 produced biographies, and these in turn are its
culture. It modeled certain life cycles, created new trajectories even
for those whom '68 just grazed because they were too young or too
old or belonged to social strata not directly affected by the student
movement.

At the root of these changes there is that "emotional stirring" of
which De Luca Comandini spoke. The direction the journey of life
takes subsequent to this is not determined, and that makes the dias-
pora more evident. There is not one fixed effect, but many. In fact, the
process is one of individuation; the more successful it is, the broader
its range of trajectories.

Thus, in the exploration of these journeys one can find parallels
and contrasts. I will give some examples. Pedro Humbert comes from
a family of tradesmen in the Po region; he attends the technical institute and begins Bocconi University. With the explosion of the movement he transfers to State and enormously expands his social life:

for someone like me, who was a provincial, to have gotten to meet
thousands of people was a big socializing factor, a sense of potential,
of being able to meet, to go to everyone's homes, without class exclu-
sions. And then this passion, yes, this passion, grew; they entrusted
me with tasks because they saw I was careful, with a rational attitude
about things and with a passion to see how the world works, how
society works, what the laws governing it are, to predict what is
happening.

In that situation Humbert develops organizational experience participating, along with other democratic teachers, as intermediate cadre in the co-leadership of classes for student workers:

> That type of political activity, beyond contributing to my personal maturation, was fruitful from a professional point of view. It was an experience, with all the lacunae I had and still have, of significant manageriality, of a real ability to manage the relationships with the teachers, in the sense of convincing them that we could guarantee [the classes], and to convince the students to continue, with the police coming in the evenings—because they kept the university open in the evenings—and then a big organizational effort to keep the whole thing together.

In this way Humbert discovers and hones his mediating skills and finds work first in a union, then in a big telecommunications company, where he attains an important position as a manager.

Mario Dalmaviva was living in Rome with his mother in '68, working as manager of a company that sold stamps, "agnostic," "apolitical," "absolutely integrated": "I cared about earning money, having a good time, that's it." One day he had followed the clashes between the police and the students.

> And I know that I had been struck, without understanding the political significance of it, impressed by the police who were beating young kids and passers-by. And this first impact motivated me to go to Paris in May of '68, but that was really a lark, that is, a week-end spent largely in the car without sleeping, to see what was going on, and it opened up a world for me. Then I elaborated everything I had seen and understood, albeit crudely, but mainly by myself, because I didn't have contacts of any kind. I experienced it as a matter of existential revolt that involved me. And mulling over what I had seen this way, in August of '68 I said good-bye to my employer and quit my job point blank. I sold the things I had in Rome, and I came to Turin on this broken-down Vespa, without knowing what I would find, who I would get in contact with, and so forth.

In Turin he found a place in the Lega Operai Studenti (Worker-Student League), "because I heard them talking about concrete things, like salaries, like workers," and he began to propagandize in front of the Lancia plant, radically changing jobs: "some used '68 to become a

manager and I used '68 to stop being a manager"; even if there was
some cross-over of skills, as he notes with the irony of memory:

> perhaps a bit of theatrical skill worked in my favor, partly inborn and
> partly honed by my profession as salesman, and so I could success-
> fully sell the things I was saying.

This last may be considered an example of reversal in the course of
life or, as the psychoanalysts say, of enantiodromia: con-version, being struck by lightening, in-version: "I lost interest in everything I had
done up to then. You know, like the guy who goes down to buy a pack
of cigarettes and comes back ten years later." A journey that will lead
to militancy in Potere Operaio, to many years of agitation in front of
the Fiat plant, and will include years in jail on charges of organizing
an armed gang and subversion against the state.

The sense of deviation from a preordained path, either taken for
granted or imagined, is frequent in these lives. It is necessary to keep
in mind that the specialness of the decade 1967–76 superimposed itself on a crucial period in the life of the individual between twenty-
five and thirty-five, the period when one usually embarks on work
and adulthood.

Lorenzo Galli, born in Naples in 1948, from a family of artisans,
belonged to the Sinistra Universitaria, then the Centro di Coordina-
mento Campana (Campana Coordinating Center), then Avanguardia
Operaia; working as a technician at Olivetti he helped build one of
the first Comitati Unitari di Base (Unitary Rank-and-File Committees). Subsequently he took out a PCI card, but his activity and identity had for some time lain in his role as union functionary. Review-
ing his life he confirms the enormous place that politics occupies:

> In '69 I was twenty-one and already my whole life was taken up with
> politics. I got married at 24–25 and continued to do the home-family
> thing and political work, all experienced within the organization my
> wife was in too. It was an overwhelming experience, of great satis-
> factions and also of great successes swallowed up in the wave of
> protest.
> Today still, in my work in the union, you continue on the wave of that
> experience: it has stayed as a sort of stamp, you carry it with you, it's
> hard to succeed in freeing yourself from it. It's a series of relationships.

On this last point there are concordances among the life histories:
notwithstanding the even violent rifts with movement comrades, net-

works of relationships developed that would persist for years; often they are still alive, especially in other cities and countries.

In these life itineraries the mixture of similarities and differences is striking; there are as many 1968s as there are individual destinies, and the mark left by the real '68 is not uniform. The process of individuation sometimes has its beginnings in '68, other times it emerges from '68 as if retarded. The woman who had participated in the movement at the State University of Milan leaves for India in reaction, where she suffers various misfortunes, including a bad viral hepatitis. On returning she joins Lotta Continua, from which she remembers "the verbosity and a climate in which you never spoke the truth." She resumes her mystical-existential search in a commune, proceeds to experiments with dieting and fasting, to the women's movement, passes through pacifist, hippy, hare-krishna cultures. (This last evokes one of her rare smiles:

> at that time you had to be dressed in pure orange or yellow or red— including underwear, socks, shoes—then you were really bizarre and seemed like one of those people who work on the highways, they could spot you from far away.)

For Marianella Sclavi, who came from an open and cosmopolitan upbringing and had already lived in Brazil and in the United States, the experience of the student movement could in certain respects represent the at least temporary rejection of a cultural identity, of plans for travel, knowledge, and study that would be resumed only much later, after the birth of a second child:

> I've never figured out if '68 was good or bad. And now I discover myself once more having the same ideas I had before '68, about a lot of important things.

The perception of a return is not the sole property of this narrator. Fiorella Farinelli also emphasizes a concept of autonomy as "recovery" of acquaintances from childhood and adolescence:

> now, after a marriage, a daughter, a divorce, and years of political militancy, I go back to Viareggio and once again visit my classmates, whom I had totally lost touch with when being independent meant the movement, collective transgression.

The return becomes a necessity of survival especially for those who have lived their experiences more from the margins:

we smashed the family, we crushed the problem of interpersonal relationships. I experienced my bisexuality, that is, I went back and forth,
I got married, I had countless female relationships and an army of the
other kind. When I talked about these tendencies of mine at the cadres-
school sessions, I got back this idea: "Fine, Communism will save you.
You've made your self-criticism and now you're cured."

In a less superficial and triumphalistic vision, someone who has
experienced his or her own multiplicity, violence, prison, does not
find simple roads for re-entering civilian life, even when, like Fontanesi, after three years in prison, he commits himself to a job like tai-
loring, which is new for him. In this reconversion it is once again a
memory older than '68 that succors and provides the strength to resume life in the present:

> Those who were the intellectuals of '68, when '68 ended they took up
> their research again, they began to write their books, their reflections.
> Those who instead were like me—I don't have anything to fall back
> on, see?
> I recovered my solid, peasant roots, these two images: death and dig-
> nity. When I went to jail, I asked my grandmother to wait for me and
> she said, "Look, I won't die 'til you get out." She died last week, a year
> since I was out, she was 91.

The experience of prison appears in the memory of Romano Madera (who spent a year, 1980, there), as an important stage on an internal level:

> There was the loneliness, there was the difficulty, the terrible violence
> among the prisoners, not to mention by the guards. However, I've
> never been so close to myself as that year. Every once in a while the
> panic of not knowing how and when it would end, but on the other
> hand being freed from the persona. I mean the mask itself, the persona
> as the side that looks out toward our exterior. Freed. Because at that
> point they had really overdone it both in the arrest warrants and in the
> newspapers: I was involved in murders, thefts, everything really. I
> hadn't done all that, fortunately. But it was also a great liberation, that
> is, you don't have anything more to defend, of the part you have on the
> outside. Now it's you and existence, you are finally yourself. In the
> meantime you are no longer yourself, but just for this reason you are
> you, because when you think there's nothing left you can count on,

you discover that there's something that keeps you afloat. You say: "But even if they take everything away from me, I consist of something."

In these lives that carry the mark of an intense season—today forgotten by most—the way one carries a secret it is always tempting to reveal (Piero Bernocchi's "you don't know who I was"), memory alternates between rage and happiness; the choices attempt to come to grips with this alternation, in order not to shatter the biography a second time, in its own recollection and in its narration.

Giuseppe Di Gennaro carried with him for years the recollection of "absolute happiness" of the first twenty days of the occupation of the engineering faculty in Naples:

> the questions of study from which we had started off seemed to us
> something wonderful, but it was really very little. By now we had
> tasted that we could really get by here, that living was not just being
> able to study better, there was plenty more!

He had gotten married, graduated in engineering, begun to teach in a high school; in the meantime he was doing organizing for Lotta Continua at the Olivetti plant, taking part in a struggle against workplace hazards. Behind all this lay the pursuit of an idea:

> that it's worth the trouble to do something in order to be happier. If it
> turns out you can't achieve this, then it starts to get a little bothersome.
> On the one hand, it bothered me to dream, on the other hand, to be too
> cautious isn't worth the trouble. . . .

> after the end of Lotta Continua I thought back to the first motion I
> had written—"the assembly must decide everything"—and I under-
> stood that this was pie in the sky. Still, the values in my life haven't
> changed, they operate through other things, but they haven't changed.

This recovery of continuity in values, through the reconsideration of the present, is something to which all the biographies tend. At the momentary terminus represented by today's stage, where there are no definitive outcomes (if they ever exist) but rather a brief pausing to reconsider the past, memory, narration, and biography reconnect with one another for a moment. For this generation what we might call the right of autobiography—to give a sense, or more than one sense, to its own past, or at least to be able to leaf through it, to unfold

it—assumes a particular meaningfulness. Perhaps we are still far
from Benjamin's piercing epigraph:

His talent is his life; his dignity that of knowing how to narrate it fully.

However, one also glimpses, next to the tones of mourning, of be-
wilderment, of uncertainty, those of the reunification between living
and narrating with the necessary detachment that allows for self-
representation without shirking the painful and unresolved points.

Romano Madera:

Naufragium feci, bene navigavi. It may be that this whole story is always a shipwreck, but on the whole I went on a great trip. Anyway,
I told myself the story like this; then the fact of having told myself the
story is no longer a simple story; it's the life I make because I told it to
myself that way.

It's also basically a slightly fetishistic idea that there ought to be something there, a social transformation, a god to encounter as something
external, and that isn't simply a story, a history: you made a life and
that life depends on how you tell it to yourself. And the life you make
now also depends on how you tell it to yourself. And the intensity that
you put into this story or into this representation is the factor that
decides whether you live a rich or a poor life, a sensitive or an insensitive life.

Peonies

7

JANUARY AND FEBRUARY

Almost by chance I begin a series of alterations in the place where I live: painting, putting in new bookcases for my books, moving things around and throwing some things away, refurbishing furniture that's in bad condition.
I understand that this is also a way of abandoning the idea of sooner or later going to live with X. But it is primarily a way of being better myself, of living in a less precarious fashion, such that it's worth the trouble to put some energy into getting settled.

I dreamed about a fruit that turned from very green to brightly colored. G. mentions his amazement at seeing something similar happening to me. Okay, I answer, some things have fallen into place, but there is still bitterness in various parts. I admit, however, that it's not going badly, that one can't have everything; and that in certain respects, bitterness is better.

The changes at home don't take place without uneasiness. I wake up at night thinking: and what if they were to evict me, after I've put in all this work? G. maintains that I would be able to enjoy it for at least two years. But the attached bookcases? He signals that they can always be moved to another house.

G. and I decide to reduce the frequency of our meetings, after a long hesitation on my part. We arrange it in advance, beginning only in April. With this delay my conflicting tendencies, to see him all the time and to liberate myself, are satisfied.
"But is it a metaphor for when we will terminate?" I want to know.

I know clearly that the journey is not completed. Now there are fewer phantoms in the space that separates us—or rather, they have been acknowledged and visited. The relationship between us is more directly in question.

MARCH

There are unresolved problems with images of the feminine. I can't manage to reconcile myself to some, and this unleashes conflicts with real women. One is the image of my grandmother, who wanted to possess me as she had possessed my mother.

With the latter, on the other hand, I speak often. I wonder what she would have been like if she had lived, and there comes to me an image similar to one of the two great-grandmothers I knew, shorter than my mother, very wise, of few words, very old. Her figure crossed with that of my mother is more ironic, she always has a little smile fluttering on her lips for the obsessions and the torments I confide to her. This mother-great-grand-mother is close to the mists of time, to the margin, to the boundary between worlds. My real mother would only be seventy-three today, while the great-grandmother I imagine would be around ninety, an age at which one can permit oneself any irony.

APRIL

The work at home is still in progress. It takes an infinite amount of time to move all the books, dust them, look at each one. I find many duplicates, I discover lost objects. The whirlwind of work is unstoppable: new curtains, or rather curtains, which I didn't have except on one window; new doorknobs; and above all—an innovation—a real bedroom, not buried in piles of books papers and documents.

I remonstrate with G. because he never contrives to give me enough advance notice of his vacation schedule.

X too has begun a real analysis, with regular appointments and with another analyst.

G. shifts one of my hours from the morning to the afternoon, to my annoyance. It's too soon, I arrive stupefied, I don't like it. The Thursday hour had been my first appointment with him, when we were trying things out to see what I wanted, it bothers me to lose it.

I mention this two or three times, but without making concrete follow-up proposals, because I think that I can hang on, only two months left until vacation. I would like to say that we could either change or eliminate that hour, but it seems like a lack of regard for G., a discourtesy.

MAY

X comes to wait for me at the end of a session. It still confuses me at times to see him; there is something of the enchanted, the miraculous—not him, but the feeling, that amazes me.

Now I understand that what seemed like a trial wasn't, it had no goal or sense beyond itself. Yes, a metaphor for the relationship with the self. And also a replay of the original wound. But not an apprenticeship that opens the door to something else, above all not to its opposite, happy and reciprocal love. Experience that counts in and of itself, as, in the old parable, digging in search of a treasure that doesn't exist breaks up every clod, disposes the earth to fertility.

Now it makes me happy to see couples with their arms around each other in the streets; I find myself regarding them with sympathy.

I dream about having another analyst, with an office like Freud's, overflowing with objects and little things, and with a couch. G. is not as impressed as I would have expected. I, on the other hand, worry about this recrudescence of my dogmatism, eagerness to have the most orthodox analysis possible, according to all the rules and regulations of the fathers.

JUNE

For three and a half years I have complimented myself on my good fortune at having found the only analyst in the world who was suitable for me. Had he been less cultured I would have despised him, had he had less of a sense of humor he would have bored me, had he been too theoretical it would have been all over for someone like me, and imagine what a disaster if he had had a prophetic or professorial tone: I would immediately have imitated him and it would have all gone up in smoke. G. was nearly perfect, except for the small defect of not deciding on the dates of his vacations. The tales of acquaintances and friends about the cruelties of analysts toward their patients had been proven untrue.

Instead the most dreadful thing happened, something I had already imagined, dismissing it for its excessiveness. G. forgot to show up for an appointment, precisely at the fateful Thursday afternoon hour I tolerated grudgingly out of regard for him. I waited a half hour, I had to accept that he wasn't coming, I phoned him, he was sleeping. I was very abrupt and circumspect, he seemed sorry.

This is a bit hard to swallow. Yes, G. explained to me the chain of coincidences that resulted in his not thinking it was Thursday. I try to believe it, suspending my old mistrust. But the most important point is that I succeeded in not giving in, as I would have done years ago. Second, in expressing my anger. Third, in admitting that the other is truly another, i.e., he has thoughts, worries, priorities different from mine. I see him as he is, for what I know about him, nor would I want to know more.

JULY

Dreams: the part of the road on which I had laboriously walked was ending, covered with snow that made my steps heavy; I was traveling a path by night, but the fog was lifting more and more and a well of white marble appeared on the path.

I don't know whether to believe in my dreams, which other times have made rash promises, then not kept them. But it was I who didn't know how to de-literalize them, to establish the right distance between night and day. It's important for the dreams to remain dreams, they don't want to be translated into daytime reality; but they do want to count.

Separation from G. This year we definitely needed a break.

AUGUST

The usual villa in Tuscany. I work on this writing, complaining to my friends about not knowing what I am producing.

I think about X on vacation with his family, but my loneliness is no longer loneliness for a man. There is no longer, compared with years gone by, the piercing nostalgia for a past. There remains a regret for politics, not for what was but for what could be, as project, as communication and community. The search for identity through the other—young people, blacks, workers, women—no longer seems to me so dissimilar from the search for the other through myself, which I have done in these last years. Not in the sense: if it can't be changed, at least I'll change myself; but in another sense: even the journey from the external to the internal, if you break the scheme dividing and hierarchizing them, can find roads for changing the world and reducing injustice.

Zaira is skeptical: you can't, she repeats to me, cast the evil out of reality, purify politics, eliminate violence from men, and from women.

I dream about a big German shepherd dog that walks ahead. He stops, forces me to stop because he wants to be petted, and he says to me a word that comes from the depths of the heart, in a deep voice: "Luisa . . . Luisa." I pet him, big seated dog, gold and black, with his head turned back toward me. The dog, encountered time and again in my dreams, who calls out from the depths, faithful mute ferocious sweet stubborn, capable of long waits, and of enjoying caresses without moving, inner dog, helmsman of other routes than that of the ego.

SEPTEMBER

On returning I find my house pleasant, colorful, welcoming. Intense perceptions, of life in the courtyard, in the city, in my rooms.

G. returns, very distracted, obligingly friendly, as if he didn't understand what I was talking to him about.

I dream about the mailboxes in the entryway: now they are of transparent crystal, but my name is written upside down.
Other dreams in sequence, in the span of a month:
dreamed of arriving in a ship on an island;
little boat through the island, guided upward by three old women (the mythological references are hardly subtle);
an old man was showing me the map of an island, with jagged coastlines. But it was impossible to read upside down. Even the lady Pope of the tarot cards holds the parchment upside down.
It is always necessary to decipher, to turn upside down, to reinterpret every presumed truth or identity. Never reached, acquired, defined.

X also resumes his analysis, which I intuit—without our ever talking about it—is star-distant from mine. Mysteriousness of these journeys. Similarities/differences in spite of the analytic schools and their rules.

London. For months Fay too has been in the process of remodeling her
house, much larger than mine. We take turns illustrating our projects for
each other, marveling at the parallels in this rediscovery of domesticity.
She too has a growing number of plants and flowers on her balconies, for
the first time she pays attention to spots on her new carpet, she is planning other changes. A French friend listens to us resigned, and reminds us
of a recent *détournement:* "In 1968 you make over the world. In 1986
you make over the cuisine."

I go to a conference at Oxford, I see friends and colleagues from many
countries again, I return enthusiastic. I explain to G., who is always float-
ing off elsewhere, but very polite, that being themselves, locals, provin-
cials, capable of insisting, is the only thing that lends substance to internationalism. On the level of cultures this is nothing other than putting
themselves back into play, throwing into the ring their own insisting. But
one can't not do both.

Pleasure of returning. Comfort of finding simpler and less threatening
food than you're forced to eat when traveling.

OCTOBER

The Andreas pass through, on their way back from travels in Europe. For
one of the two it is Paris that once again has unveiled fantastic things
about the world and about himself, that has revived writers and poets as
comrades in work and kin in suffering. For the other it is Berlin; the wall
has violently shaken the traveling group of young people, but while some
spoke of bombs to blow it up, he experienced it as those irremovable
things that are found within oneself, those wounds or mutilations one has
to pay attention to.
Amazement, consolation at hearing things experienced come to life again
with new accents. The emphasis on subjectivity is new. I too remember
that a long time ago Paris had been a place for delving into torments; to
me too the wall appeared, even just a few years ago, like a fissure in the
heart of Europe. But they talk of Paris as of their own room, and of their
own heart as if it were that of Europe—or perhaps it is my ear that has
learned to hear.

If Federico de Luca Comandini is right, if under the immense confusion
we go from a historical and collective consciousness to an individual and
subjective one—through reactions in the opposite direction, of exagger-

ated reification as well—there is still something to examine and to pursue. Incorrigible tendency to make sense of history.

Fay's daughter also passes through, much bigger than Fay and different, maybe more like her father, whom I don't know because they have been separated for many years. But I detect in this big adolescent her mother's quick sparkling leap from one subject to the next, her auto-ironic theatricality.

Long letter from Eric, who is leaving again for another long tour of Africa. Nostalgia for our conversations; who knows when we will resume them.

NOVEMBER

Arguing with X I confirm his impatience. He snatches every opinion contrary to his own out of thin air and crushes it, with irresistible zeal; his adversary often retreats not out of fear but out of regard, since to oppose him would lead to a frontal assault: he takes every dispute personally. If I still felt animosity—or if it were not under control—what used to happen continually in my first semiconjugal relationship would happen: a free-for-all between two aggressivities. And yet each of us had put the other at the center of our lives. Maybe I can no longer have anyone at the center of my life nor be the center for someone else.

Enough of the revisitation of fixed roles: mother/*puella*/heroine/Griselda, enough. Slim down, lighten up.

Everything continues with some repetitions—variations on a theme. Perla brings her new baby for me to see. Sonia exhibits a sort of eclectic secular mysticism and studies the Kaballah. Perla worries about the damage done by excessively strong mothers, perhaps she is afraid for herself as well; she reasons about it with me and finally reassures herself alone: "It's not that we're not strong—she associates me with her strength—but fortunately we have found men, and women, who oppose us."

G. and I talk of hardly anything other than this manuscript any more, so much does the question of what it is preoccupy me. Will it become a book? And if not, what is it? something internal to the analysis, an anthology from the countless notebooks of my analytic diary, to recapitulate the journey and give me the sense of continuing it? and if so the objective chapters would be abortive essays, to be rewritten and outfitted with notes so that I can publish them in specialized journals?

I am continually divided in one sense or another: at my work table I reread my writing and find it shameful, full of pettinesses; I go away from it
and in the course of the day some good passages come back to me, it
seems to me, on the whole, interesting. Or vice versa: I enjoy myself and
am enthusiastic about writing; I go to sleep and have to get up in the night
to mark out insipid sentences. But when I get to my table and reread
them, I find they have a certain grace, if not a complete sense, and I stop,
uncertain. It happened the other night with two passages on the peonies
in the third chapter.

G. takes up the defense of the peonies. He too once wrote a poem with a
line about them. He also defends the right of someone who has another
job and knows it, doesn't want to abandon it, to be a poet. I fear the ridiculous, bad literature; I don't like to fall short of the mark in my professional identity, I wonder if silence isn't better. I assure G. that this writing
project did not belong to the ego, that in fact the ego has often opposed it
and is a bit ashamed of it.
G. insists that the problem arises because I am thinking of publishing the
manuscript, rather than considering it written primarily for myself. But he
doesn't convince me.

Christmas approaches. Zaira, pitiless: "Your usual flight abroad?" Actually I do have some trips in mind, places I have been wanting to go for a
long time.

DECEMBER

Forgot for the first time to telephone X. Recurring dreams of huge piles of
snow that melt and break up into running rivulets; dreams of returning, of
circling the castle, circumnavigation of the mountain and landing in the
valley.
This book is finished. I can begin once more to do serious things, like
methodological essays with footnotes and copious bibliographies. I am
content to return to my trade, I have various projects in mind. However,
I'm sorry to abandon this manuscript, to let it go. It had already separated
from me, when it occurred to me to call it a "book," something I had
never done: it becomes something other than me, with an independent
life, whether flourishing or barely surviving I don't yet know.
I see now how forceful the process of selecting the most appropriate segments and reordering them has been, in the transition from the original
diary to this version. I am struck by the margins of invention writing has

permitted itself, by the transformations in order to guarantee anonymity or to render the actual recurrences of living, such as the fusion of different people with similar roles. Writing it has been wonderful; it was my vacation this year. I am distancing myself from it very rapidly, and as the distance grows the characteristics of elaboration and construction appear to me more and more distinct, those of revelation or confession more and more irrelevant. This wasn't the issue, and thus it didn't require any particular courage, such as would be necessary to tell the whole truth and nothing but the truth.

The ego breathes a sigh of relief and regret simultaneously, its adventure is over too. It behaved with courage, accepting sorrow and joy, the cowardly part and not just the rebellious part of this undertaking. The id is quiet, sly, it sends little riddle-dreams, hints at unforeseen solutions. All together, like a merry troop of actors, we are reasonably well disposed to accept what will come, the next piece of writing, for as long as we can.

Turin, July-September 1987

AUTHOR'S NOTE

The odd-numbered chapters are the liberal elaboration of a diary kept during the years 1983–87; the sections in italics make use of two long interviews by Roberta Fossati and Claudio Novaro, and some previous autobiographical writings: *"Diario di militante"* ("Diary of a Militant"), *L'erba voglio,* 16, May–June 1974; *"E continuavano a chiamarci femministe"* ("And They Still Called Us Feminists") (with other authors), *Sottosopra,* 1974; *"Desideri"* ("Desires"), *Sottosopra,* 1975; one of *"I percorsi"* ("The Journeys"), *Memoria,* 19/20, 1987. The "objective" book mentioned, the fruit of an international research effort, is R. Fraser, D. Bertaux, B. Eynon, R. Grele, B. le Wita, D. Linhart, L. Passerini, J. Staadt, A. Tröger, *A Student Generation in Revolt,* Chatto & Windsor, London, 1987.

The even-numbered chapters are based on a collection of interviews, completed during the same period, with the following individuals (the cities in parentheses indicate where each one experienced 1968):

Franco Aprà (Milan)
Franco Barbagallo (Naples)
Piero Bernocchi (Rome)
Luigi Bobbio (Turin)
Mario Dalmaviva (Rome-Turin)
Federico De Luca Comandini
   (Rome)
Luciano Del Sette (Turin)
Laura Derossi (Turin)
Paola di Cori (Rome)
Giuseppe Di Gennaro (Naples)
Vittorio Dini (Naples)
Roberto Dionigi (Paris-Bologna)
Fiorella Farinelli (Pisa)
Maria Teresa Fenoglio (Turin)
Helder Fontanesi (Bologna)

Franca Fossati (Milan)
Lorenzo Galli (Naples)
Agnese Gatti (Trent)
Nadia Ghesini (Bologna)
Pedro Humbert (Milan)
Paolo Hutter (Turin)
Romano Madera (Milan)
Cesare Marconi (Rimini)
Diego Marconi (Turin)
Eliana Minicozzi (Naples)
Momo (Naples)
Guido Morbelli (Turin)
Renato Musto (Turin)
Maria Nadotti (Milan)
Serena Nozzoli (Milan)
Peppino Ortoleva (Turin)

Ettore Pagani (Milan)	Franco Russo (Rome)
Irene Palumbo (Naples)	Marianella Sclavi (Trent)
Franco Piperno (Rome)	Marino Sinibaldi (Rome)
Luigi Refondini (Milan)	Mariella Tagliero (Turin)
Marco Revelli (Cuneo-Turin)	Anna Tratteur (Turin)
Dario Romano (Milan)	Guido Viale (Turin)
Marco Rostan (Rome)	Vittorio Vidotto (Rome)

This list should also include two individuals who have chosen to remain anonymous (Naples, Rome). I wish to express my heartfelt thanks to these interviewees; their contribution to this volume goes far beyond the quotations that appear in it. Daniel Bertaux, Patrizia Guerra, Bruna Peyrot, and Paola Sobrero conducted seven of the interviews; I conducted the other forty. Lidia Sinchetto transcribed them; I have made stylistic revisions to the quoted passages.

Chapter 4 makes use of documents regarding Turin 1968 consulted at the Fondazione "Vera Nocentini" and the Centro Studi Piero Gobetti di Torino and in the private archives of Luigi Bobbio and Diego Marconi.

Chapter 6 utilizes life histories collected during a seminar held at the Turin New Prison in the winter of 1986–87 (Nadia Mantovani and Susanna Ronconi) and interviews with Silveria Russo by Patrizia Guerra and with C.R. by Domenico Nigro, both conducted in the context of a research project on "Political Violence in Italy During the Seventies," directed by Raimondo Catanzaro for the Istituto Cattaneo di Bologna.

Also important for me were the preparatory discussions for a cycle of accounts on "Public and Private in Turin '68: Women's Experiences," which took place in the context of my course on historical research methodology at the University of Turin; Franca Balsamo, Donatella Barazzetti, Betti Benenati, Laura Cima, Laura Derossi, Gabriella Filippi, Victoria Franzinetti, Santina Mobiglia, Anna Nadotti, and Eleonora Ortoleva participated in these discussions.

ABOUT THE AUTHOR

Luisa Passerini was born in 1941 in a small Piedmontese town. She studied at the University of Turin and traveled widely, spending long periods of time in the United States and Africa. She participated in the Italian New Left and in the feminist movement. She is now professor of History of the Twentieth Century at the European University in Florence. She has written a number of books on Fascism including *Fascism in Popular Memory* (1987) and edited *Memory and Totalitarianism* (1992).

ABOUT THE TRANSLATOR

Lisa M. Erdberg is a former practicing international tax attorney turned italianist. She graduated from Radcliffe College (1969) and has a Ph.D. in Italian from the University of California at Berkeley. She has taught at the University of California at Berkeley and at the Museo ItaloAmericano in San Francisco.

LIBRARY OF CONGRESS CATALOGING-IN-PUBLICATION DATA
    Passerini, Luisa.
        [Autoritratto di gruppo. English]
        Autobiography of a generation : Italy, 1968/Luisa Passerini ; translated by
    Lisa Erdberg.
            p.   cm.
        ISBN 0–8195–5286–0 (cloth : alk. paper)
        ISBN 0–8195–6302–1 (paper : alk. paper)
        1. Italy—Politics and government—1945–1976. 2. Italy—Social conditions—
    1945–1976. 3. Baby boom generation—Italy. 4. Social change—Italy.
    5. Students—Italy—Political activity. 6. Passerini, Luisa. I. Title.
    DG577.5.P38513   1996
    945.092–dc20   96–15984